CRUEL CITY

THE DARK SIDE OF
HOLLYWOOD'S RICH AND FAMOUS

CRUEL CITY

THE DARK SIDE OF HOLLYWOOD'S RICH AND FAMOUS

Marianne Ruuth

ROUNDTABLE
——— Publishing, Inc.———

Library of Congress Cataloguing-in-Publication Data

Ruuth, Marianne.
Cruel city / by Marianne Ruuth.
p.   cm.
ISBN 0-915677-48-2 : $19.95
1. Public relations—Motion picture industry. 2. Hollywood (Los Angeles,
CA.)—Social life and customs. 3. Motion picture actors and
actressess—Biography—Miscellanea. I. Title. PN1995.9.P79R88 1991
659.2'93848'0979494—dc20   90-52813
CIP

FIRST EDITION

10 9 8 7 6 5 4 3 2 1

Photographs are from the private collection of the author.

In turning the world upside down I sometimes think that Freud more than anyone else must have been astonished to find that it tended to remain upside down.

—Henry Miller

It's a funny old world and a man's lucky to get out of it alive.

—W.C. Fields

For Joanne

who walks in beauty

TABLE OF CONTENTS

CRUEL CITY

THE DARK SIDE OF
HOLLYWOOD'S RICH AND FAMOUS

CHAPTER 1

Hooray For Hollywood

Hollywood, the Press, and Public Opinion

They wait, often in long lines, to experience another dimension. Having entered a darkened room, they sit in rows, faces turned upward. One concentrated area on the wall in front is lit. The spectacle begins. Larger-than-life figures, more real than life, appear. Faces, several feet high, come close, revealing the reflection in the pupil of the eye, the widening of the nostrils. They are laughing, crying, orating, making love, sweat drops glistening on foreheads, breasts, buttocks. Bullets and knives leave gaping wounds, showing the blood, the pain, sometimes the death, of those who are brave, cowardly, impressive, frightening, alluring, just as gods should be. They don't have bad breath or sticky hands. They do what gods—and artists—should do: they awaken the primitive, anarchic instincts which have been sacrificed in a society striving for comfort. They also act as a magic mirror in which the viewer sees his dreams and nightmares.

What is the continuing relationship between the main figures in the modern mythology and those on whose emotions they play? What does the symbiotic bond do to each?

An actor pointed out the close similarity between going to a place of worship and a movie theater the other day, adding, "That's why, when an actor walks down the street, people either want to kill him or hand him a governorship!"

Since it is easier to take man as a symbol than a fact, and, since the fine actor never seems to act but *be*, is it any wonder that many filmgoers believe that Hollywood stars are the characters they portray, heroes, cowards, sexy or

1

evil? Early in the history of the film industry, its leaders
admitted to this fact, and set their stars to adhering to the
illusion. This included living a highly moral life, strictly defined by studio codes.

At any rate, that's how it was to appear.

In 1919, diminutive star Mary Miles Minter's public
image was one of purity and innocence. As such, her contract with the Realart Company (Adolph Zukor of
Paramount) would, for the term of three-and-a-half years,
pay her $1,300,000.

Aside from the usual terms, the contract concerned itself largely with the star's intimate life and mode of living.
She was not to become a "public figure," except in the way
her employers directed. She could be interviewed by the
press only at the discretion of the Realart executives, and,
even then, was to follow their explicit directions. She was
seldom to be seen in public. The contract defined her appearances, her statements, her acquaintances—as well as
her work. Additionally, she was not permitted to marry for
the term of the contract, evidencing the control the studio
was to hold over her private emotional and sexual life as
well as her public one.

The contract demonstrated a valid distrust of the media, notably the Hollywood press.

The relationship between Hollywood film studios and
the press has, at best, always been an uneasy "marriage of
convenience." The attitude of the movie moguls who established and ran the movie studios well into the 1950s was
one of virtually total paternalism. Almost from the beginning, the press found it convenient to respect their wishes,
since they controlled most sources of information. The
Hollywood press would reveal anything that was rumored
about one actor while zealously guarding the privacy of
another. Some private lives were laid bare, while others
were carefully shielded. The alcoholism and drug addiction
of film stars were almost always overlooked by the press,
unless a star's contract was being dropped and it was no
longer necessary to abide by the studio's sanctions.

Barbara Stanwyck was one of the "untouchables,"
while a star such as Hedy Lamarr was shooting gallery
game; you could write anything about Hedy and get away
with it. Many did.

Stanwyck never signed a long term studio contract,

such as Bette Davis did at Warner Brothers or Joan Crawford at Metro-Goldwyn-Mayer.   Extremely independ-
dent—and with a firm belief in what she would or would
not do—she signed only one or two picture deals, never
remaining at one studio very long. As a result, she never
accumulated the studio publicity support that most major
stars enjoyed.   Ultimately, she would pay the price by
never winning an Oscar, an event preceded by a barrage of
studio publicity.   Neither did she have the publicity protection that her contemporaries, such as Bette Davis, Joan
Crawford, Ginger Rogers or Loretta Young, had.

Stanwyck had something better: Helen Ferguson.
Ferguson's petite prettiness belied a formidable woman
willing to avidly protect her clients' privacy—especially
that of Stanwyck.

Helen Ferguson had been a silent and early talkie film
star (she was the little girl with the long curls and big eyes
in some of the Rin Tin Tin movies). In the 1930s, she
started her own public relations firm.   Two of her first
clients were Barbara Stanwyck and Robert Taylor before
their marriage. Taylor remained with her until he died;
Stanwyck until Helen retired because of ill health in 1970.

For over thirty years, the only way the press got to
Stanwyck was through Helen. They were close friends and
Helen remained a constant bulwark between "Missy" and
any unfavorable publicity. When, in the early 1950s, Stanwyck and Taylor divorced, it was Helen Ferguson who
originated and perpetuated the story that Stanwyck remained in love with Taylor until he died.   In actuality,
Stanwyck, Taylor, and his second wife, Ursula Thiess, were
on good terms. The "still in love" story, however, kept the
press from delving into Stanwyck's personal life. The Barbara Stanwyck who the public knew was the Stanwyck
Helen Ferguson wanted it to know. The public Stanwyck,
actually, was only slightly more mysterious than the private
Stanwyck.

That was true of all the clients Helen Ferguson represented. Never numbering more than six at any one time,
the personae she created for her clients were based closely
on their real personalities. Helen Ferguson was a nice person; her clients were nice people. That way, there were no
surprises along the way, no shattering secrets. If Taylor
was less than a perfect gentleman, or Barbara's language

could occasionally make a sailor blush, Helen's relationship with the press meant that the press looked the other way, now and then.

When they appeared, rock stars were not so lucky.

As a group, the press had nothing against rock and roll, but, generally, rock performers were young and inexperienced with the press when they became, almost overnight, stars. It took longer to become a movie star, and most who reached that status had long since learned that some behavior would not be tolerated or go unreported.

Today, the film industry is, for the most part, run by corporate boards of directors with little personal interest in the people who turn out their product beyond the bottom line of the profit and loss statements. With their computerized studies in demographics, they tend to become upset if an article or photograph defines a movie before its publicity release date, for which they may punish the offender by denying access to stars or screenings.

Not so in the days of the movie moguls—never a class act themselves—who utilized the press as a bouquet, a whip or, at times, a knife. Many times, a powerful individual would have the press deliberately distort a story—even to the point of destroying a career—in order to achieve a contractual or personal demand. Under instructions, the press would traditionally join hands in a silent conspiracy to protect certain stars and certain studios, while they happily fired away at others. At other times, anything deviating from a desired image would be carefully and efficiently removed.

Rock Hudson's death in 1985 from AIDS illustrates this point, and, finally, changed some media attitudes.

Even though the press certainly knew the facts, a former bit actor and stuntman who had been involved in movies for twenty-five years would state that he had actually worked with Hudson and never suspected, nor heard, nor read anywhere, that he was homosexual. Throughout his career, Hudson, a gentleman and loyal friend to many, had been protected—first by the studios and, finally, by a valiant press.

When it comes to homosexuality, the unwritten rule has long been accepted by the mainstream press that a star must conceal his sexual preferences. The assumption was that the awareness of a homosexual tendency would change the audience's perception of his or her image, even to the point of alienating moviegoers.

In recent years, however, a phenomenon called "outing" has occurred. The term simply stands for "out of the closet," and has found favor among many homosexual rights groups throughout the country. In a business that deals with images, the term strikes a note of terror, arousing considerable concern. Much discussion as to the necessity of publicizing the sexual orientation of an actor—or any public or image figure—has created highly visible walls of disagreement. Certain segments of the gay press feel that a celebrity who conceals his or her sexual leaning is doing a disfavor to other gays. Some would like to see more gay role models among the rich and successful.

"We want to get away from the idea that homosexuality has to be kept a dirty little secret," has become their battlecry.

The tabloids especially feed on outing stories, acknowledging that they sell papers like no other stories, even those about a son or daughter of a star or the lurid, descriptive recollections of former bedmates of the famous.

"We think only of the readers," is the tabloid defense.

Some journalists find it grossly unfair. "How are some of these actors going to get jobs as leading men?" one reporter asked. "Who would dare to cast an outed gay as the male lead in a love story?"

Sandra Bernhard, the outspoken comedienne, tends to shrug when the tabloids write about her, but still finds it "grossly irresponsible." "They're fascists," she says about the tabloids.

Certainly, this kind of publicity hurts gay men more than gay women. The public seems to be able to ignore such revelations about female stars more than males.

In the early days of film, outspoken Tallulah Bankhead gave a magazine interview in 1932 in which she said she was perfectly able to have a love affair with any man an hour after meeting him.

The silent alarm sounded.

The Hays Office nervously appealed to major newspapers and magazines not to print that part of the interview and the star, the editor and the reporter were threatened with reprisals. The dominos neatly fell into place—except that the beautiful Tallulah herself shortly thereafter deserted Hollywood for the legitimate stage. Her studio expressed no regrets. Tallulah's notoriety was in constant conflict with the image they were vainly attempting to create.

At the end of the 1920s, the famous Malibu Beach colony came into existence specifically as a place where stars could play, drink and entertain out of the sight and hearing of the gossip collectors.

Hollywood, however, is nothing if not flexible when it is convenient—or lucrative.

By 1926, a heavy decline was being felt at the box office. Reasoning that sex, scandal and sensation could be used creatively to whet the appetites of moviegoers, the moguls began a series of selective titillations, limited, however, to certain stars. Certainly a handsome leading man could not be injured by stories of a multitude of sexual trysts or a bad boy image damaged by a traffic violation.

But this applied only to some stars. The old moral standards stayed alive for others.

Dorothy Cummings, who had played the Madonna in DeMille's *The King of Kings,* discovered the double standard when she sued her husband for divorce in June of 1927. Lawyers argued that under her contract with Cecil B. DeMille—signed the year before—she must so regulate her life for seven years that not the slightest reflection might be cast on her character, "thereby to prevent any degrading or besmirching of the role she was about to play."

The contract spelled out the penalties in some detail:

"Because the people of the Christian faith are sensitive concerning their faith and are anxious that no reflection, direct or indirect, be cast upon Christ or his Mother in particular, during the seven years designated as the life of *The King of Kings*, Miss Cummings must conduct herself with the regard to public convention and morals, and, at all times, must observe and act in entire accord with strict Christian conduct and behavior."

Cummings   contended—successfully—that   such   a

clause was an infringement on personal liberty.

Yet, as late as 1965, when Max von Sydow was cast as Christ in *The Greatest Story Ever Told*, the actor had to agree to forego press interviews and live an extremely circumspect life with regard to smoking, drinking, and other personal habits, at least until shooting on the film was concluded.

The message was clear: no conflict of images.

Elizabeth Taylor's screen roles and off-screen life and temperament have definite similarities. The public visualizes Taylor as a somewhat mythical figure, even in her minor films. Taylor has survived the studio image to become a modern star, bound to no studio and, consequently, master of her own life and career. She is one of the stars whom the public will forgive anything, largely guided in their sentiments by the press. For most of her career, Taylor has been a favorite of the press and the public.

Even the tabloids have to be careful of going too far in Taylor's case. Generally, she has ignored their headlines, but, when she was reported as drunk—when she was actually very ill and required round-the-clock nursing—she filed suit against *The National Enquirer*, a supermarket weekly that claims a circulation of over four million. It immediately became apparent that members of the mainstream press were on Taylor's side. After her critical illness early in 1990, her suit attested to the fact that she had been pushed around enough for one year and public opinion was definitely on her side. *The National Enquirer* immediately filed counter motions, seeking access to examine Ms. Taylor's medical records for the past thirty years. The paper also sought to transfer the suit to a Federal court. Other tabloids, heeding public reaction, retreated to the subject of Taylor's weight.

The media tends to swing between looking for perfection and searching for feet of clay, even though the scandal sheets may, at times, seem to provide proof that their particular audience prefers sin to virtue.

Many editors feel their star interviews must have "bite." The suggestion is that an idol must have at least one clay foot, even if it has to be fabricated.

A symbol of virginity, such as Doris Day, is "boring,"

say many editors. Give us a Dorian Gray, with a gorgeous outside and a dark inside. No one knew Hollywood like actress-turned-columnist Hedda Hopper: "Nobody is interested in sweetness and light."

Gossip is not a modern phenomenon. A sixth century Byzantine historian named Procopius published a private collection of spicy gossip about public figures called *Anecdotes* (from the Greek word *anekdotos*, meaning "secret, not given out").

During the 1960s, the "find the warts technique" manifested itself heavily:

- An editor in New York felt that an article about Frank Sinatra lacked "bite," so he made up a dirty comment and put quotation marks around it.
- An article writer, who couldn't get an interview with Red Skelton, sneaked a tape recorder in Skelton's dressing room and recorded a number of lines—non-funny, never meant to be heard, and certainly never meant to be printed.
- John Wayne was slated to do a series of articles under his own name. After the first interview, the writer called and informed Wayne he much preferred to do the rest without Wayne's cooperation. Wayne's comments lacked "bite."
- Janet Leigh was threatened—as were several stars—that, if she didn't submit to a magazine interview, the magazine would do an article based on the most tasteless and ugly rumors it could find.

Eventually, some powerful stars would follow Sinatra's example. Asking why he should hold the axe that was aimed at his throat, he demanded to read articles before they were submitted for publication.

Even that axe had a double edge, however. Stars who insisted on censoring articles found them so white-washed that they lacked any color or interest.

Some had no problem. Jack Lemmon states, "I'm dull copy. I lead a simple, quiet life. Is it more important that it is readable, or that it is the truth?"

Many stars sigh and assume the classical attitude, "Let them write what they want as long as they spell my name right." Others remain sensitive to what is said and written about them.

In many cases, stars have received riches and attention to such an extent that they themselves are unable to understand the phenomenon. In some cases, they believe they couldn't possibly deserve it and panic, worried someone will find out just how undeserving they are. They do prefer those scribes who are as star-struck as any fan and act as nice interpreters of handfed publicity material.

A lot of nonsense has been written, and continues to be written, about Hollywood.

In all fairness, it is almost impossible *not* to fall into a certain glossiness at times when writing about stars. If a god smiles at you, how can you resist describing the godlike qualities in such a way that the god will smile at you again?

Vicious as they may seem, today's supermarket tabloids are still a far shout from the most famous of the scandal sheets, *Confidential*. In a magazine which concentrated on controversial dirt-digging, bona fide reporters, masters of innuendo, moonlighted as writers or informants. The studios themselves often fed it stories, sometimes to punish a recalcitrant performer, more often to kill another story which would damage one of their own properties. Many a minor star would be sacrificed to protect a major property. A story about Rory Calhoun's jail sentence for robbery was swapped for an expose on a major star's appearance in a homosexual bar.

Universal Studios had both Rock Hudson and George Nader under contract when the studio learned that *Confidential* intended to run an article on Hudson's homosexuality. The studio arranged a deal in which Hudson's story would be cut in exchange for cooperation on a similar story involving Nader. The story ran and just about killed Nader's career.

Confidential employed private eyes as informants. While the rest of the media accepted the publicity releases concerning the amicable split between Marilyn Monroe and Joe DiMaggio, *Confidential* featured an article on how Frank Sinatra and DiMaggio had gone to 754 Kilkea Drive in West Hollywood to trap Monroe with a lover. Only after they had physically broken down the door did they discover that they were at the wrong house.

Confidential's headlines illustrate the magazine's expertise at innuendo and guilt-by-association:

A young woman named Tyna English revealed that Warren Beatty was overrated in bed. The article included the floor plan of Beatty's Beverly Wilshire hotel suite.

In the same issue, another woman, Monet Teray, revealed that "Movie Mogul Jack Warner bought me for a summer of sex!" followed by Mickey Hargitay's revelation that his former, late wife, Jayne Mansfield, "played the violin in the nude." A few pages later, one of Hollywood's worst kept secrets got another play with "Cola Queen Joan Crawford spikes her Pepsi" with booze.

The next month found Laurence Harvey the "Homosexual Darling of the Jet Set" and revealed that Loretta Young, Judy Garland, Hedy Lamarr, Lana Turner and Eva Gabor had all supposedly recently had facial plastic surgery.

The following month, Tommy Smothers was reported as having kissed the belly button of someone named Nancy Burton. The issue also revealed that Frank Sinatra had driven his former son-in-law, Tommy Sands, crazy and that Sands was in a Hawaiian rest home as a result. The article reported that Sinatra could not stand the idea of a happy marriage in the Sinatra family. In the same issue, readers were informed they could get syphilis from a public telephone.

A following issue again spotlighted Sinatra as "Sinatra—A Misfit and his Money" by Tracy Cabot. Sinatra was great to listen to, but no one wanted to live with or near him, it was proclaimed.

Sinatra had good reason for his paranoia concerning the press.

In subsequent issues, readers were informed that "Marilyn Monroe was a Lesbian," which was a spinoff of the Sinatra/DiMaggio break-in with a "known lesbian" named Sheila thrown into the picture; "Brigitte Bardot's bust, butt and boys were all sagging;" Nixon was cheated out of being president in 1950 because Lyndon Johnson controlled the voting count in Texas; Peter Sellers got a divorce because he was "afraid of sex;" Bob Hope "fixes beauty contests"; and "oral sex kills women."

Later, *Confidential* revealed that someone named Anne Gardner got "burned by monkeying around with Peter York;" that Alain Delon's friends "are murderers, pushers and blackmailers;" that Michael Caine had been "voted man of the year by 10,000 prostitutes;" that rock music turned teenage girls into "phallus freaks;" and that Nancy Sinatra had recently had her "boobs blown up."

To round out the year, *Confidential* wanted to know if Tom Jones's crotch was "real or padded?"

While stars were embarrassed, and sometimes hurt, MGM responded to *Confidential* by making the movie *Slander*, with Steve Cochran, Van Johnson and Ann Blyth. Cochran portrayed a sleazy, magazine publisher and Johnson played a television star being blackmailed. The movie ended with the editor's own mother shooting him for being "unfit to live."

Tom Wolfe noted that it wasn't the lawsuits that put *Confidential* out of business, it was the stars. Beginning with Hedy Lamarr, they started telling their own stories.

In April, 1933, Joan Crawford sued Douglas Fairbanks, Jr., for divorce. That *same week*, *Modern Screen* hit the stands, its cover blaring "The Exclusive Inside Story of the Joan-Doug Separation." Lead time—the time magazines require between the writing, editing and typesetting of a story, plus transporting it to the newsstands—was no less than two months at the time. So—who leaked that story, so perfectly timed? Even today, some stars feed tidbits to the tabloids, deny it as they may.

The early fan magazines were important to the studios, since they served as advertisements for their products. At a time when daily newspapers and major magazines gave minimal space to movie personalities, *Motion Picture and Photoplay*—both established in 1911—were read by millions of young people, the movies' prime targets. In order to secure the right kind of stories, however, the studios required that these magazines sign a pledge of "clean, constructive and honest material."

Of course, there were always mavericks. *Close Up*, a tabloid created by Jaik Rosen, who began his career as a Hedda Hopper legman, was little more than an excuse to carry on Rosen's personal vendetta against those he disliked.

"If they have chosen Hollywood, they deserve what they get," was his motto. In the manner of today's tabloids, he utilized the services of spies all over Hollywood—cigarette girls, waiters, cab drivers, bartenders, masseurs, maids, errand boys, and anyone who could supply him with information.

From his miniature army of spies, Rosen received tips and items of "news," which he then presented in his cynical manner. Among his milder reports: Adolph Menjou's cigarette case with the inscription "To Adolph Menjou from his greatest fan, Adolph Menjou," and Stewart Granger's habit of sending congratulations to his mother every time he celebrated his birthday. Rosen also intimated that Granger always showered in cold water, so that steam would not cloud his image in the mirror.

Tabloids print stories and stars sue. Movies and records are made and groups protest against immorality or scatological language; some manage to get banned or labeled—which may or may not hurt sales. Some instances would be funny if they weren't frightening: in 1990, in Culver City—the home of Metro-Goldwyn-Mayer—the children's book *Little Red Riding Hood* was banned from the school's library because Little Red Riding Hood brought her grandmother wine and, even worse, grandmother felt good after she drank it.

Today's movies have fewer restrictions than in the past. In 1939, David O. Selznick was fined $5,000 for allowing Clark Gable is use the word "damn" in *Gone With The Wind*. Far from breaking new ground in the movie industry, the word was not heard on the screen again until 1954 in *On The Waterfront*.

Recently, movie ratings have fluctuated wildly, and with no seemingly logical sense of reasoning. Mild cases of sexual exposure seem to take precedence over severed heads and mutilated bodies. The "X" rating was replaced by a rating that no one—including moviegoers—understood. The simpler times are gone. When Samuel Goldwyn was warned that Lillian Hellman's *The Children's Hour* was about lesbians, he supposedly made a corporate decision, "Don't worry. We'll make them Americans." And another movie mogul praised a picture as being very modern because the words 'sex relations' were used six times.

On the whole, filmgoers seem to follow the adage that "Motion pictures have ruined a lot more *evenings* than they have *morals*."

But the public's appetite for stories about and

glimpses of the stars remains unsatisfied and the media continue to portray Joan and Liz and Tom and Mel larger than life, in one way or another, for better or for worse shaping them into fantasy figures.

And the stars are often caught up in their own images, seduced by their own legends.

Stars become accustomed to seeing and hearing themselves described in superlatives; fans scream and faint at the sight of them; particles of their clothing are ripped off and treasured. It is remarkable that any of them remain well-adjusted. The mental climate of Hollywood has never been conducive to intellectual or emotional maturity.

Stars become dazzling entities, forced into narcissistic existences and constantly enticed by the siren songs of everyone around. Assuming them to be experts on anything and everything, caught up in a mirroring attempt at adulation, the public—and often the press—expect too much of them.

Like most of their adoring public, a great many stars have neither more or less of an opinion on much of anything. A few are not smart enough to make up their own minds—much less the public's—about any issues, although some are very bright, intelligent and well-read.

In a recent television interview, a marvellously candid, educated and intelligent Katharine Hepburn, who has always been more interested in world affairs than Hollywood gossip, confessed than she has never been particularly proud of the way she made a living, since an actor was not required to be very smart or even very talented. "Shirley Temple did it very well at the age of five," she remarked.

The Hollywood book of rules contains one maxim: a star is someone to whom nobody tells the naked truth.

Neither is a star someone about whom the naked truth is told.

Instead, a star is someone who resides somewhere between the truth and complete fabrication.

Mention the name of Fatty Arbuckle today and, if remembered at all, only one fact has survived: the death of a starlet named Virginia Rappe in a San Francisco hotel room. Most Hollywood residents have known and repeated the story for years. What most don't know—or seem to care about—is that Arbuckle was acquitted. Deserted and fired by his studio, Arbuckle, along with his wife and close friends, would spend the rest of his life maintaining his innocence. The Hollywood gossip circuit, however, aided by a vicious press, convicted him of manslaughter in the public's mind.

It was Labor Day weekend, 1921. Roscoe C. "Fatty" Arbuckle, the baby-faced comedian, weighed 350 pounds. Originally from Smith Center, Kansas, he had worked his way up from being a singing waiter, playing in stock companies and burlesque revues, to becoming one of the country's most beloved comedians.   Together with director Freddy Fishback and actor Lowell Sherman, he headed for San Francisco for a few days of fun and relaxation. They stayed at the Hotel St. Francis and decided to throw a party to celebrate Fatty's newly-signed $3-million contract, which confirmed his position as king of Hollywood's silent screen.

Among those attending the party was a young girl named Virginia Rappe. Newspaper accounts at the time called her a film actress, a starlet, and a film extra. Years later, film historians would even state that she was a call-girl. During the party, Rappe complained of stomach pains. A few days later she died in the Wakefield Hospital of a ruptured bladder.

And so it began. Rumors were first whispered, then spoken louder and louder that Arbuckle had raped the girl with a champagne bottle and crushed her beneath his weight.

Some witnesses testified that Rappe had accused Arbuckle of having injured her. Defense witnesses stated that Rappe had a couple of drinks, then went into another room in the suite and began tearing off her clothes and screaming. Several women guests were said to have put her into a tub of cold water, thinking she was having an attack of hysteria.

Tabloids around the nation portrayed Arbuckle as a pervert and the public outcry against him forced his films to be withdrawn from circulation by distributors. Ultimately, he was fired by Paramount. Meanwhile, Arbuckle was jailed without bail for weeks. His lawyer's first move was to try to reduce the charge to manslaughter and the comic was led from his cell in handcuffs. Shortly before her death in 1975, his wife, Minta Arbuckle, who did not accompany him to San Francisco, described the trial:

"There was one woman in the crowd, the head of a vigilante women's group, who had a lot of her followers with her. As soon as she saw Roscoe, she said, 'Women, do your duty.' And they all spat at Roscoe."

On April 12, 1922, after three sensational trials, a San Francisco jury acquitted Arbuckle. But the verdict had little effect on the public.

The Arbuckle affair, along with the unsolved murder of William Desmond Taylor and the dark glimpses into the lives of the movie people involved, had the public enraged. Hollywood was dubbed "a graveyard of virtue" and it was implied that William Hays, head of the censor board, had been employed only to whitewash the film industry's immoralities.

Even the judge at Arbuckle's trial would stress, "What we are trying here is our present day morals."

Arbuckle was a free man, but there was no contract with Paramount Studios and his notoriety had made him unemployable. Also, the dominos had begun to fall because of his arrest. On July 12, 1921, a district attorney of Middlesex County, Massachusetts, was accused of taking bribes for not proceeding against some prominent movie people involved in an embarrassing affair at a Boston hotel on March 6, 1917. The bill for the night, $1,050, included the entertaining of twelve young women who later lodged complaints and were quickly paid off. Adolph Zukor had attended the party, but the guest of honor was Fatty Arbuckle.

His screen career gone, Arbuckle attempted a nation-wide vaudeville tour, beginning his act by pleading his innocence, "I want to go back to work. I want to make people laugh. Yet I can't come back. They won't let me."

According to Minta, his attempts to rally public opinion were futile and failed miserably. His career was over. Jack Warner let him direct three shorts, but he was unable to use his own name. The name he used was Will B. Good.

Arbuckle managed to get a one week vaudeville engagement in Long Beach, California in 1924, but a local association of ministers petitioned the city council to have his appearance cancelled. Arbuckle appeared before the council, pleading that he owed $184,000—the cost of his trial. The majority of the council was moved by his personal plea and allowed him to perform.

In 1925, Minta and Arbuckle were divorced. Following a disastrous European tour in 1932, he returned disillusioned and died of a heart attack at the age of forty-six.

As a result of the Arbuckle scandal, Universal Studios issued an announcement that it had inserted a morality clause into all present and future contracts with its stars. Any act that offended the community or outraged public morals and decency would lead to a five days' notice of cancellation of the contract. Other studios gradually followed suit.

The forgotten piece of the Arbuckle puzzle is Virginia Rappe. The young girl of Swedish descent, who lived in Hollywood and tried to become a star, was only one of the many faceless and nameless hopefuls. Henry Lehrman, who directed some of Arbuckle's films, had taken an interest in her and had brought her to the Hotel St. Francis party.

Would she have made it?

At that time, fifty Hollywood studios were employing twelve thousand people. The annual payroll was forty million dollars. Screen Service, an agency for extras and bit players, had more than 100,000 applicants listed, of which four or five managed to get substantial roles and only one male star emerged. The Chamber of Commerce released a poster showing 35,000 individuals showing up in response to an advertisement for thirty-five extras. According to the *Literary Digest of 1924*, Hollywood was "the port of disappointed youth."

It still is.

CHAPTER 2

Why Actors Are the Way Actors Are

From the beginning of the film industry, it has been the actor that has held fascination for the public, not the screenwriter, who creates and develops the seed of a story nor the director who nurtures that seed into maturity. Instead, the actor has been the center of attention, concentrated to the point of adoration. That adoration is emotionally dependent, to a degree, that the fickleness or devotion of the public may rest entirely on a brief moment of memory.

On the retention of fame, film historian Richard Griffith once remarked, "The emotional binge of stardom leaves its victims in a state of perpetual hangover."

A leading Hollywood psychiatrist stated, "Actors are basically lonely individuals who hunger to relate to others. They are scoptophilic, meaning 'lovers of looking.' They look and hear very keenly. Their lovers and mates have a tough time with their main rival, the audience. They [the actors] love the audience and are scared of the audience. And audiences love to see someone who is doing, albeit on the screen, all the things they would love to do, but don't dare to do. At the same time, there exists a contempt in the minds of many in the public because the actor is, after all, pretending. In order to be a star, a person must have an enormous drive for acclaim. Often, these individuals come from disrupted homes, and a great number of stars were neglected, abandoned, even beaten as children."

As a young child, Jay North starred in the popular television series, "Dennis the Menace." In later life, North would reveal in an interview that, during the filming, his aunt and uncle—his guardians at the time—would beat him and threaten him "if I took more than two or three takes to get it right."

"This town takes kids and destroys them. The agents destroy them. The parents destroy them," he stated, damning Hollywood.

North revealed that it took years of therapy, as an adult, to allow him to cope with the effects of abuse, depression and substance addiction.

North is certainly not alone. Actors were among the first to look to the psychiatrist to help them with their problems. At one time, there was one psychiatrist for every 169 residents in the film colony. The national average was one for every 13,652 persons. One street in Beverly Hills had so many psychiatrist offices that the residents dubbed it "Libido Lane."

Early Hollywood stars succumbed easily to the images created by themselves or their studios. Female and male stars freely shared time with starlets and rising beach boys in front of the still photographers cameras, often spending hours posing for picture spreads which would be packaged for individual magazines. Ego was tolerated by a studio in much the same way a tantrum by a small child would be. Stars survived by being smart, knowledgable or cooperative. With the control of the media well in hand, Hollywood studios fed the public and the nation what they wanted it to believe.

But, with the rise of television, the world began to mature and the level of insight and knowledge of the individual viewer began to broaden. Early screen goddesses, such as Jean Harlow, Lana Turner and Joan Crawford had existed for their careers, allowing for little else in their lives. What publicity their studios allowed was either crushed (as in the case of Crawford) or splashed deliberately across the tabloids (as in the case of Turner). Both cases were cleverly designed to aid the career of the particular goddess.

However, at the beginning of the 1960s, a change in attitude began to occur. Obvious differences existed between the young screen goddesses and the old.

"I really love my work. Right now, it's my whole life. But I'm not sure that will always be true . . . the right man could easily become the most important thing in my life . . . if he asked me to give up my career, I know I could do it," Faye Dunaway stated.

Ali MacGraw stunned her fans with, "I want to be myself and not just a movie queen."

The stars of the modern American movies were obviously a different breed from their forebearers. Even the offspring of the old guard had their own ideas. "I still can't make up my mind whether acting is for me, or I for it," Candice Bergen announced in 1969.

The new breed of Hollywood stars tend to deny their abilities, rather than stress them, almost to the point of *hubris*, the Jewish belief which would invite doom for bragging of one's achievements or possessions. Pia Degermark achieved stardom and stated in an interview, "I had a very happy life before *Elvira Madigan* came along. I could never make being an actress the pivotal point of my life." She subsequently gave up her career.

Early in film history, someone compared fame to being inside of a hall of mirrors, where all you can see are myriad distortions of self, self, self, self...

Among those not officially famous, there is a fantasy about fame. The religious mystery of immortality may be the ultimate appeal, projected by movies and their stars. The motion picture itself is an interestingly contradictory phenomenon in that it combines the *motion*, the constant change, with *picture*, the unchanging, frozen image. And in movies you stay young forever, you live forever, and fame seems to mean being loved, accepted, seen, noticed, envied. Even though the term "star" indicates someone orbiting above the rest, being unreachable.

George C. Scott narrowed his sights on Hollywood when he stated, "Self-loathing sets in when you realize that you are enjoying [fame] . . .What is ultimately so harmful is that you are being recognized, not for the things that you worked so hard for, but for other reasons—that you are a movie star, for instance. After a while, the pleasure stops, but the self-contempt stays."

"How can they love me," one actor exclaimed. "They don't know me. They love that image—what I represent—not who I am."

The nature of the human being is to have gods. Having

given up on the gods of mythology, filmgoers seem to be attempting to recreate them in film stars. But film stars are also human beings, trying to cope with normal lives and passions at the same time as they portray abnormal ones. The paradox is often confusing to the idolizer, but can be deadly to the star who is unable to differentiate between the two lives he is living.

Many psychiatrists stress that living with an imaginary image of oneself, and feeding that image at every opportunity, may eventually result in an inability to contact one's actual self. Nothing but the image is left. The real person could be left unattended.

Many actors have submitted to psychoanalysis before, during or after being an actor. In many cases, specialized forms of acting technique deal directly with truth and an actor's ability to deal with the truth of a character while creating a role. So-called "method acting" has been sinned against by those who believe that it preaches an actor must "become" a part, while, in actuality, it stresses that an actor must find identical truths in both himself and the role and match them.

Patrick Swayze expresses his thoughts as an actor, "I've always been wrecked with emotion and very insecure all my life. I think that is your job as an actor—to keep yourself insecure. One of the first things you learn in an acting class is to break the pictures—the images—you have of yourself, because if you see yourself as macho or quiet or shy or gay or angry or intellectual . . . it limits the wealth of other characteristics you have inside . . . I shot down my ego to a fault. I'm better at it now in terms of not destroying my insides and keeping myself in a state of very low self-esteem.

"When you go way down inside and start opening and playing with that Pandora's Box, it gets very dangerous. In many cases, you should have a license to do what you're doing."

Many actors are loath for the public to discover their true selves, primarily because their true selves are a mystery to even themselves. When it comes to self-discovery, they are as unsure about themselves as other "normal" beings. The constructed image seems safer.

In interviews, many stars state that they grew up wanting to be someone else. They have now achieved their desire. However, should they look for admiration, they find admiration for the image they have created, not for the self they have abandoned. They are not loved for who they really are.

Woody Allen's comical quote penetrates to the bone, "The other day a man came up to me and kept saying over and over again, 'You're a star! You're a star!' I thought, this year I'm a star, but what will I be next year—a black hole?"

If that admiration truly disappears, many find the image disappears as well, and nothing remains of their original self. Only an empty shell exists and, often, a star will abandon the shell—in one way or another. Suicide in Hollywood has never been uncommon.

Samuel Goldwyn did not worry about psychiatry, self-esteem or imagining. He simply stated, "God makes stars. It's up to the producers to find them."

The stars Goldwyn and other movie moguls found are a many-faceted group, ranging from the suicidal to the ridiculous, from the intellectual to the stupid, from the beautiful to the ugly, and from the egotistical to the naive.

In their flippant, off-hand or quoted remarks, they inevitably reveal a little of themselves. Jack Carson once quipped, "A fan group is a group of people who tell an actor he's not alone in the way he feels about himself."

"[Hollywood] will pay you ten thousand dollars for a kiss and fifty cents for your soul," said a beleaguered, tired Marilyn Monroe.

Lord Laurence Olivier, a soul-searcher as well as a perfectionist, described his profession, "Acting is a masochistic form of exhibitionism. It is not quite the occupation of an adult."

But adults they are, and, as adults, some attempt to demand respect, while other surrender themselves to the images they have created in their search for fame.

In a *Time* magazine interview, Jerry Wald once capsulized the Hollywood dream:

"It's the same story with different names. First, they say, 'If only I could get a part.' After they get a part, it's 'Gee, they like me! I wonder if I'm gonna get another part?' Then comes phase three: 'I should be getting bigger and more important parts.' After that: 'How can I get more money?' At this stage, they start to become surrounded by sycophants and suckerfish who feed on the whole, who massage their ego. In the next stage, they're frightened: 'I have to make lots of money now. How long can I last?' Then comes the stage where they're like a roman candle. They've reached the first plateau. Everybody wants interviews with them. . . They're invited everywhere.

"The stage after that is when they become a mature star and accept everything. They stop pushing. That may take two or three years. The next stage is to break from the friends who disagree with them. Then comes the phase when they need help from someone, so they change agents and boyfriends. There's a lot of constant insecurity.

"The final phase is where they get culture. It's the 'I was listening to Beethoven's Ninth the other night.' . . . The names may change, but the anxieties and pushing and disappointments are still the same. They're all reaching for the biggest jackpot in the world."

Director George Sidney put it simpler:

"I say you take a normal person—your Aunt Matilda—and put makeup on them, and it affects their brain. I say to the makeup man, 'What have you got in that stuff?'"

It may seem as if the Hollywoodites exist in a world of their own, though everyone may not carry it as far as Louella Parsons did. When Hitler invaded Albania in 1939 and the world was holding its breath, teetering on the brink of disaster, Parsons noted, "The deadly dullness of last week (sic!) was lifted today when Darryl Zanuck admitted he had bought all rights to Maurice Maeterlink's *The Bluebird*."

It must be noted that Hollywood consists mainly of hardworking, thinking, enormously talented people who do have an impact on the world; they are bearers of gifts of inspiration, of understanding; they may amuse or disturb. Already, Thomas A. Edison, who helped to make it all possible, wrote, "I consider the greatest mission of the motion picture is first to make people happy. . . to bring more joy and cheer and wholesome good will into this world of ours. And God knows we need it."

The early film makers knew the ultimate power of movies. Cecil B. DeMille observed, "It is a sobering thought that the decisions we make at our desks in Hollywood may intimately affect the lives of human beings—men, women and children—throughout the world."

Today's actors are more aware of social issues than ever, truly concerned with what a movie has to say, and wish to be seen as *actors* rather than stars. Consequently, they are unwilling to give up their privacy, avoiding intrusive publicity with the words, "All I really owe the audience is the best performance I am able to give." If they are left alone by the press, however, many feel abandoned and threatened in this city of contradictions.

CHAPTER 3

When Dreams Turn Into Nightmares

Barbra Streisand once said that while an artist is struggling, he or she is ignored; if the artist makes it, there is spontaneous applause; then, if the artist stays on top, there are two possibilities: he or she becomes "boringly normal" in the eyes of the press or some kind of monster which makes for good copy. Boring or bad—not a terrific choice! Even worse is to become a joke, the real career killer. Looking back in time, Clara Bow went through the adoration, the hate, and finally became a joke. Some very obscene jokes went around at her expense.

Hollywood called Clara Bow the "It" girl. "It," referring to a very powerful sex appeal, was coined by Elinor Glyn, a popular novelist of the 1920s. Clara Bow is a prime example of a personality the press adored to the extreme and eventually turned on, tore down, and hated to the same extreme. Clara was a tense girl, fond of playing jazz music very loudly, who gave one the feeling that she had to hurry because there was so little time . . . so little time . . .

Adela Rogers St. John, who interviewed Clara at length, wrote that "there was no peace in her." The reporter also related how Clara Bow spoke of her birth—the doctor predicted it would cause her mother's death.

Clara's childhood had more than one touch of the macabre. Her grandfather dropped dead as he pushed her in a swing. A little neighbor boy was burned to death before her eyes. Her mother fell more and more a victim to insanity, and once tried to slash Clara's throat claiming life was too brutal. When her mother died, Clara, still a child, tried to jump into the open grave.

At the age of sixteen, Clara entered a movie fan magazine's beauty contest. There were ninety-nine other girls in the competition, well-groomed and beautifully turned-out. Clara arrived with her carrot-red hair, her baggy sweater and cotton stockings. The other girls whispered and snickered about her, which awakened her fighting spirit.

The girls seemed not to notice the prettiness of her face or how gorgeous her dark eyes were. Twenty girls were chosen for a screen test. Clara was among the winners. She proved to have a natural sense of timing, no doubt fostered by going to the movies every chance she had.

Five girls were chosen from the screen tests. Then the choice narrowed to two girls. Then, the winner—Clara. Her prizes were a silver cup, an evening gown and a bit part in a movie, *Beyond The Rainbow*. But sadly her part ended up on the cutting-room floor. When she landed another small part, Ben Schulberg spotted her and sent her a ticket and a promise of $50 a week if she would come to Paramount in Hollywood. In 1925, she signed a contract with Paramount Pictures. Even in small parts, she made big impressions. "When Clara Bow is on the screen, nothing else matters," one critic wrote.

At Paramount, she was molded into the symbol of the flapper, with bobbed hair and lips shaped like a cupid's bow. In 1927, she starred in the movie, *It*, written by Elinor Glyn. Hence the epithet and her immense popularity. Her love affairs, involving Gilbert Roland, Gary Cooper, Victor Fleming and a host of others, contributed to her popularity, though she had her own code: "No married man in my bed." The newspapers and fan magazines reported her love affairs in great detail, often mixing fact and rumor, creating an odor of scandal. According to those who knew her well, Clara was smart and sweet, although terribly scarred on the inside by her childhood with its lack of love.

It is ironic that Clara Bow's perpetually readiness for wild parties, her flirtatious behavior, and disregard for convention made her the idol of the flapper era. But, when her off-screen life became an extension of her movie roles, she was condemned by the press.

Paramount even had a morality clause which guaranteed her a bonus of $500,000 at the expiration of her contract, if she did not "run wild" in public.

But, toward the end of the 20s, Clara became involved in several scandals, including an alienation of affection suit which cost Paramount nearly $30,000 and lost her that bribe for good behavior. The wife of a Dallas physician sued Clara for having alienated her husband's affections. The bad publicity increased, especially after she went to a Nevada casino and lost $14,000, paying it off by check, and later stopping payment. There were also unsubstantiated reports that she had entertained Al Capone in her studio dressing room.

Paramount tried to salvage the situation, since Clara still had several months left on her contract. In a movie entitled *No Limit*, she played an outrageously flirtatious woman, trying to absorb her real life situation into her screen image.

But the ploy did not work. She took the public's rejection hard and, never having been strong and healthy, suffered both a physical and mental breakdown. In 1931, she sought the care of a psychiatrist, after her secretary, Daisy De Voe, had betrayed her hard won trust and written checks for a fur coat, a house and other luxuries for herself.

Clara sought a refuge from her life and married Rex Bell, the cowboy star. They lived on his Nevada ranch. Although she appeared in two movies after her marriage (*Call Her Savage* and *Hoopla*), she retired permanently at the age of twenty-six.

The marriage produced two sons. Rex Bell was twice

elected Lieutenant Governor of the State of Nevada—but Clara Bell was seldom able to enjoy her new family life. Depression and severe insomnia constantly plagued her and she spent years in various sanatoriums, reportedly gaining weight. She died at the age of sixty, apparently of a heart attack, while watching a movie on "The Late Late Show." At the time, Clara Bow had become a recluse, living in a world of her own.

Silent screen idol John Gilbert also died of a heart attack—but he was only forty-one years old. He had become a heavy drinker, partly due to the nagging frustration of a brilliant career soured by the advent of talking pictures. It went deeper than that according to several sources—here was a celebrated actor who actually hated acting.

John Gilbert was the biggest male star of his day—the screen's Great Lover, the successor to Valentino, and the co-star of Greta Garbo. His salary was $10,000 a week, then $250,000 a picture. Suddenly, he was utterly ruined, finished—ridiculed. The reason, according to the story most often told, was that when he opened his mouth to speak words in his first "talkie," people laughed. Humiliated and increasingly desperate, he tried to drown his doubt and remorse in drink which led to an early death.

Is that the truth?

Partly.

In a *Photoplay* article dated September, 1928, he wrote, "I became a famous personage. Everywhere I went, I heard whispers and gasps, in acknowledgment of my presence . . . 'There's John Gilbert! Hello, Jack! Oh, John!' The whole thing became too fantastic for me to comprehend. Acting, the very thing which I had been fighting and ridiculing for seven years, had brought me success, riches and renown. I was a great motion picture star. Well, I'll be damned!"

His real name was John Pringle. His father was a stock company actor/manager, and John began his career on the stage. He quit early because he had an eye on making movies, not acting in them. At the age of twenty-three, he was signed to a five-year contract ($1,500 dollars a week, plus half the profits) to direct films that would glorify the protégé, Hope Hampton, of multimillionaire Jules Brulatour, who held the controlling interest in the Eastman Kodak Company. The first film was a total disaster. John, who, at the time, was madly in love with Leatrice Joy, one of the most elegant stars of the silent screen, simply tore up his contract and fled 3,000 miles west to California. His lack of money forced him back into acting—screen acting.

Gilbert always maintained that he despised acting—perhaps this was just an affectation. He fought with directors—his temper flared up easily—after which they would go out for a drink and promise lifelong friendship.

He had a tendency to become immersed in his roles to the extent that he had trouble keeping his private personality independent of his image on the screen. He tried to live his roles off-screen as well.

So, why then did he not make it in talking pictures? His voice may not have been great, but neither was it as high-pitched as claimed by some film historians. Perhaps it was that the reality of talkies was immensely different from the silent films. The Great Lover who has no voice lives in one's imagination. When he suddenly spoke, his audience may have felt . . . embarrassed.

Film makers learned from Gilbert's failure to soft-pedal dialogue in romantic love scenes, so perhaps we all owe a debt to John Gilbert.

There was more than one side to the personality of Gilbert. Bosley Crowther, in his biography of Metro-Goldwyn-Mayer mogul Louis B. Mayer, wrote that, shortly after *The Big Parade*, Gilbert casually remarked to Mayer that his mother was a whore. Mayer was horrified and jumped on the actor, pounding him with his fists, until others pulled them apart. Since that incident, Gilbert was held in scorn by Mayer, the man who held his career in his hand.

Gilbert's last few years were difficult ones. The studio

tried to salvage Gilbert's screen image by changing it. In *Way For A Sailor* (1930), he played a hard-boiled, hard-drinking sailor who takes love lightly. "His voice isn't all that bad," reported *Variety*. But audiences did not take to this new Gilbert and the effect was shattering to the actor. It was as if he were left alone without an identity, as if his very masculinity, his deepest self had been ridiculed.

He was married to Broadway actress Ina Claire from 1929 to 1931. She gave him voice lessons, but these lessons made him feel even worse: to be an object of pity.

The Phantom of Paris (1931) was not a bad movie, but when he appeared in *West of Broadway* (1932) it became obvious that the studio was handing him inferior roles so that he could work out his contract. For *Downstairs* (1932), he wrote the script and co-starred his new wife, Virginia Bruce. It was a bitter film. The role he wrote for himself was the role of a man who goes in for blackmail, conmanship and double-crossing.

In 1933, Garbo demanded him as her leading man for *Queen Christina*. It seems to have been an act of friendship and loyalty. Gilbert was the one who gave Garbo her first big break by approving of her as his co-star in *Flesh and The Devil* (1926). Now Garbo was able to repay the favor and she did. The studio had wanted John Barrymore for the part. Garbo said no. She also rejected Nils Asther, Fredric March and newcomer Laurence Olivier, and insisted that John Gilbert play the part.

Shortly after *Queen Christina* premiered in New York, in the early days of January, 1934, a twenty-eight-year-old man named Herman Cline, whose father was chief of detectives in Los Angeles, fell—or jumped—from a hotel window in Denver and was killed. In an obituary in a film trade paper, Cline was reported to have dubbed the voice of John Gilbert in some of the actor's films. Cline's death occurred a few hours after he had to stop his nightclub act—ironically because his voice had cracked.

Gilbert's role in *The Captain Hates the Sea* in 1934 was one that was close to him—a burnt-out and self-loathing writer, who goes on a sea cruise to try to stop drinking and begin writing again. Gilbert drank heavily throughout the shooting of the film. A few months later, John Gilbert was dead from a heart attack.

"The girl is too beautiful," was the billing in her Hollywood films. As the Roaring Twenties began, Barbara La Marr was a dancer who was discovered for a part in *The Three Musketeers* which starred Douglas Fairbanks.

She was strikingly beautiful—the comparison with Elizabeth Taylor has been made—with satin-black hair and blue, almost violet, eyes.

Her real name was Reatha Watson. She eloped and became the teenaged bride of a wealthy young rancher, got an annulment, and, the next year, married a young Los Angeles lawyer. The morning after the wedding, her groom was arrested. The charge was bigamy; he already had a wife and three children.

Devastated, she concentrated on her dance lessons and became a sensation at the 1915 World's Fair in San Francisco. She married her handsome dancing partner, but, shortly thereafter, the police arrested him on forgery charges. He was sentenced to San Quentin.

Barbara felt guilty; he had showered her with expensive presents.

Then came the turning point.

The Three Musketeers made her a star. Her beauty made audiences gasp.

She was happy, wrote screenplays, made movie after movie. But her private life turned increasingly chaotic. Paul Bern (who later married Jean Harlow and then killed himself) tried to commit suicide when Barbara suddenly married an Irish actor, giving her as the reason. Even after her wedding, other men pursued her, causing her husband to feel constantly jealous.

The love affair between Barbara La Marr and the press also went sour. They had adored her, but she was now being treated with suspicion. It was reasoned that a girl that beautiful and six times married had to have loose moral standards.

Confused by the treatment of the press, Barbara drank more, used cocaine, and slept less and less. She went out with just about anybody, as if to demonstrate that she did not care. In 1926, Barbara La Marr died in a sanitarium, a victim of alcohol and an overdose of drugs. She was twenty- eight years old.

The studio announcement, which the press dutifully reported, was that Barbara had died from "having dieted too rigorously."

For the period, she had the perfect figure. By today's standards, she was already a bit overweight and soft. Marie Prevost was a popular star of silent movies and early talkies, getting her start as a Mack Sennett Bathing Beauty in 1917. She stayed with Sennett until 1921, then she joined Universal Pictures, where she became a leading player in romantic film comedies.

Three Ernst Lubitsch-directed films constituted the peak of her film career: *The Marriage Circle*, *Three Women*, and *Kiss Me Again* made in 1924 and 1925.

By the mid-1930s, her career began to wane, primarily because of an increasing weight problem. The motion picture camera adds pounds, so the perfect figure had to be slim as an exclamation mark. Marie desperately wanted to continue her career and went on an extremely harsh diet. Eventually, she stopped eating altogether. On January 23, 1937, in surroundings indicating extreme poverty, she was found dead in her home. Her pet dachshund was moaning pitifully by her side. Bites over her entire body showed that the dog had been trying to awaken his mistress—who had been dead for several days. The cause of death was listed as extreme malnutrition. Marie Prevost was only thirty-eight years old.

Mary Nolan was called "The White Flame." She was a woman other women loved to hate. She and Lupe Velez were close friends until Gary Cooper entered Lupe's life. Lupe Velez was not going to take the chance of Coop even seeing Mary Nolan.

Fair-haired and lovely, she was born on December 18, 1905 as Mary Imogene Robertson and was raised in a convent. Appearing in the *Ziegfeld Follies*, where she was enormously popular as "Bubbles," Mary Nolan had admirers by the score. Scarred by a beating she received from an actor, she fled to Germany, where she starred in several motion pictures. In 1926, she returned to America and Hollywood and was seen in fifteen movies, ending with *The Midnight Patrol* in 1932.

However, she did not enjoy Hollywood. Her outrageous statements ("to kiss John Gilbert is like kissing a relative") and her blatant flirting made women freeze her out. She was bitter about Hollywood, the people in show business and, finally, the public. She turned to religion, claiming to have visions and to have had intimate talks with God. Mary Nolan disappeared into obscurity in 1932 and died— alone—a few years later.

"The Most Handsome Man Alive", the reports stated. In any case, Wally Reid was something special as far as masculine looks and charm were concerned.

Reid became the world's supreme matinee idol. Not only were his looks those of a Greek god, but he could act, had musical talents as a composer, singer and violinist, wrote poetry and drove his own race car.

Born April 15, 1891, he made his stage debut at the age of four. By the time he was nineteen, he had moved into films playing the blacksmith in *The Birth of a Nation*. He was soon Paramount's leading male star. His mentor was Cecil B. DeMille, whom many critics, including Adela Rogers St. John, would blame for Reid's downfall.

Reid had been happily married to Dorothy Davenport since 1913. She co-starred with him in many films and they had two children, Bill and Betty. DeMille would constantly make Reid feel that his natural loving and kind nature, his

desire for one love and a harmonious one-on-one relationship with his wife was "ridiculous, childish and unsophisti-
cated."

By 1919, Reid's popularity was at its peak. The press
adored him and followed him around Hollywood as he
drove a convertible, blue as a robin's egg with a horn that
played "Yankee Doodle Dandy."

He seemed to have it all—including a heavy dependency on morphine.

One source claimed that Reid suffered severe head
injuries in a train crash and was given morphine for the
pain. Another stated that a giant redwood tree crashed
near him during the filming of *Valley of the Giants*, and
that he was given morphine for the blinding headaches
that resulted.

In either case, Wally Reid became an addict.

By 1922, his condition had deteriorated so much that
he was placed in a sanatorium, where he died in tremendous agony and suffering in a padded cell at the age of
thirty-two.

The news of Wally Reid's drug addiction did not break
until a Hollywood drug ring was exposed and his name was
found among its records. The scandal rocked Hollywood.
Such posthumous revelations had serious consequences
when it was revealed that racketeering existed in the movie
colony, supplying heroine and cocaine to the stars.

Paramount fought the press, emphasizing how bravely
Reid had struggled against his addiction. His widow even
appeared in *Human Wreckage*, a story which dealt with the
physical and moral breakdown of a young lawyer as he becomes addicted to narcotics and is brought to ruin and
death.

If David Ward Griffith, the trailblazing pioneer who
co-founded United Artists and created magic never before
seen on the screen, did not die young, the tragedy of his
death began early and festered for many years.

His career began its downhill plunge in the middle of

the 1920s and he made his last movie in 1931. By the time he died at the age of seventy-three, he was a sad and bitter man, drinking heavily, sitting at the back of modest restaurants, needing a shave and a clean shirt. He would reach out desperately for a temporary audience to whom he could tell his past glories.

"I never had a day's luck after Lillian left me," he was quoted as saying. Lillian was Lillian Gish and the truth was that she did not leave him; he left her. Obsessed with a starlet named Carol Dempster, a pretty, but not overly talented actress, Griffith dropped Gish, who was the moviegoing public's dream girl.

His career illustrates his monumental mistakes. He made *Dream Street* with Dempster and filmed *Orphans of the Storm* with Gish, who remained with him professionally even after their romance ended. *Dream Street* was a resounding flop; *Orphans of the Storm* is still hailed as a work of art. Yet, D. W. Griffith continued making films exclusively with Dempster and success continued to elude him.

The man the press referred to as "The Father of the Movies," was a lonely and forgotten man when he suffered a cerebral hemorrhage in his hotel room at the Hollywood Knickerbocker Hotel on July 23, 1948.

Charles Ray died from an impacted tooth at Cedars of Lebanon Hospital in Los Angeles on November 23, 1943.

He was once known as "Ince's Wonder Boy" and seemed to be the embodiment of the American country boy.

Born on March 15, 1891 in Jacksonville, Illinois, Ray's family moved almost immediately to Los Angeles. He studied business in college, but always wanted to act, and put on playlets wherever and whenever he could. In 1912, he heard that Thomas Ince was hiring actors. He took a Red Car (The Pacific Electric InnerCity Cars) to Ince's studio and was hired as an extra. Noticing his naturalness before the camera, Ince cast him in *The Favorite Son* and signed him to a contract. By 1917, Charles Ray was one of the brightest stars in Hollywood.

"I like country people," he said. "Maybe that is the reason I gravitated naturally towards my characters. These country boys are the very spine of the nation. They come to town full of hopes and plans, and they grab at life like a pup grabbing a thistle, and they don't let go when it stings. They just grab harder. At last, they get the job they want, and the girl they want, and they get a little polish without losing their clean country ideals. I like them, because they are Americans—just as the screen is distinctively an American art. You can't find their type anywhere else in the world."

In 1921, Ray began directing his own films such as *A Tailor-Made Man* and *The Girl I Loved*.

But, a few years after, America's country boy had lost his appeal. Ray could not accept this; he sank all the assets he had and everything he could borrow into a movie he felt glorified the birth of America, *The Courtship of Miles Standish*. The public failed to respond. The picture was a financial disaster, leaving Ray broken, owing money everywhere. Even on the brink of bankruptcy, he hosted a fabulous party and invited everyone involved in any of his films. He had engaged a string orchestra and the champagne flowed freely.

Ray and his wife had to move from their Beverly Hills mansion into an inexpensive, small apartment. Everything went to auction. Clara Ray opened a dress shop on Sunset Strip. Ray's career was virtually over except for an occasional part.

One man still believed in Ray—Thomas Ince. He cast him in the movies *Dynamite Smith* and *Percy*. But, when Ince died, Ray made few films. *The Garden of Eden* was his last important role. He moved to New York, tried the Broadway stage without success and wrote a play that was never produced. When his wife divorced him, Ray remarried and returned to Los Angeles and had a few lines in Cary Grant's *Ladies Should Listen*, ironically in a part of a man looking for work. Four years later, at the age of forty-seven, Ray was given a bit part in *A Little Bit of Heaven* by a casting director who heard he needed work. The contrast between the star he had been and his present reality as a bit player threw Ray into a dark depression.

When Ray died, Louella O. Parsons wrote, "I think Charles Ray died of a heartbreak that began many years ago when, broke and discouraged, he realized his bright, particular star had set, and that there was no comeback."

Warner Baxter broke into the movies during World War I. His big break came in 1929 with his first talkie, *In Old Arizona*, when he assumed the role of the Mexican bandit, The Cisco Kid, from actor/director Raoul Walsh when Walsh lost an eye in a car accident.

Attractive, and with a great speaking voice, Baxter was a popular star. His success continued through the 1930s and early into the 1940s, when he suffered a nervous breakdown. But Baxter continued working, particularly in the popular *Crime Doctor* series. He was plagued by arthritis and, at the age of sixty in 1951, he underwent a lobotomy in an attempt to cure the condition. However, the operation was complicated by pneumonia which led to his death.

The diminutive star of *Shane*, Alan Ladd, died from an overdose of sedatives combined with alcohol. A little over a year earlier, he had almost died from a self-inflicted gunshot wound. Both events were labeled accidents. Pulled between conflicting emotions of not wanting to desert his family and serious career disappointments, Ladd's accidents could have been no more than that.

Ladd was plagued by an immense, gnawing insecurity during his whole life. He never quite understood how he had gotten to where he was. As a child, he had shown a burning desire to excel and, in spite of being only five feet four-and-a-half inches tall, he was an outstanding athlete in high school, becoming both a swimming and track champion. Ambition led him through menial jobs to the apprentice program at Universal. He appeared on screen for the first time in *Once In a Lifetime* (1932).

Aided by his second wife, Sue Carol, an actress turned agent, Ladd kept climbing higher and higher on the ladder of success. Rave reviews for his acting were few and far between however. In his first big success, *This Gun For Hire*, he died with his head in Veronica Lake's lap. Tradepaper *Variety* wrote, "Better men have died with their heads in less pleasant places." But the public liked the tough-fisted, tight-lipped man with the sculptured, immobile face. *Shane* (1953) brought him to the top. Alan Ladd was just fifty years old when he died at his Palm Springs, California home on January 29, 1964.

Carmen Miranda, the Brazilian Bombshell who added spice to many Hollywood films during the 1940s and 1950s, is said to have died of a broken heart at the age of forty-three—although the medical diagnosis was peritonitis. Though she seemed never to give up, Hollywood began to ignore her in the 1950s. In her last movie, a Dean Martin-Jerry Lewis comedy, *Scared Stiff*, she was referred to in the media as a has-been. Today, Carmen is best remembered for her "fruit capote" headdresses—and for a photo taken during a dance sequence on the set of one of her films. Carmen is being twirled around, legs high, by her leading male dancer. When the film was developed, it showed that poor Carmen had worn no undies that day.

Beautiful Florence Marly deserved a better fate. In the beginning, she had it all, then, through a clerical mistake made by an inept United States government employee, it was all taken away from her. At the very time she was achieving a breakthrough to becoming a major star, she was falsely accused by the McCarthy House of Un-American Activities hearings of being a communist and was subsequently blacklisted by the film industry.

Florence Marly was one of the most mysterious

women in the world. Born in Moravia, she was a French citizen who, during her life, lived in Czechoslovakia, France, Argentina, Japan, Chile, and Mexico. She ended her life in the exclusive suburb of Westwood, near the UCLA campus.

While still a student at the Sorbonne, where she studied art, literature and philosophy, Florence was discovered by French director Pierre Chenal and rushed into her first movie, *Alibi*, only a few days later.

"I was so young," she recalled in a 1972 interview. "I didn't know what it all meant. I had always wanted to be an opera star, but I didn't have the voice for that. I had never seriously thought about a film career, and, if I had, I certainly had never voiced such a desire. In Moravia, the theater was not thought of as a respectable means of earning one's living.

"After entering the Sorbonne, other students would tell me that I should be in films because they thought I *looked* like a film star.

"Actually, I had never seen a film star in person. To me, the films were another world, a dream where everyone was very, very beautiful—or so much more beautiful than I considered myself to be. I thought of them as some creatures from a distant planet. I knew nothing about makeup, and had never seen a camera until I was directed by Chenal in my first scene."

Alibi launched Florence's career in France and the press soon dispelled any doubts she might have had about not being beautiful enough for films. The press hailed her as "the most beautiful girl in the world." *Alibi* was quickly followed by such great French films as *L'Affaire Lafarge, Cafe de Paris*, and *Les Maudits*, the first film directed by Rene Clement. *Les Maudits* won Florence a best actress nomination and the "Best Motion Picture" award at the Cannes Film Festival for Clement.

Then Germany invaded France. She continued working as the Nazis advanced on Paris.

"Oh, how I hated the Germans then because of what

they had done to my own country—and were doing to my adopted France. And how very young and foolish I was at the age of twenty. I intended to stay in Paris and spit on the first German soldier I saw. Of course, I would have been shot.

"Fortunately, I escaped from Paris, but not until the day before the Germans moved in. And what a story it is of my escape! I was in my apartment, doing nothing. Waiting, I suppose, for the Germans, when Marie Bell, the actress, telephoned me. She screamed when she learned I was still in Paris, with the Germans only a few miles away. She knew how I felt about them and the trouble I'd get into if I remained in Paris. 'Escape! Escape!' she shouted over the telephone.

"Well, I still had my car. It was a new Packard and had not been taken by the government because it burned too much gasoline. All French cars had been taken to use at the front, but not foreign cars.

"What a day! The skies were black because they had burned all the gasoline deposits to keep it from the Germans. I remember looking out my window at the skies dark with smoke and Marie Bell screaming, 'Leave! Leave now!'

"Then she suggested I take two women she knew who had no way to get out of the city. One of them was Jewish. Such strange women they turned out to be. At the time, I knew very little of life, otherwise I would have been wise enough to escape Paris weeks before—as had almost everyone I knew. But, young and foolish as I was, I suspected something was not right with those women. It wasn't until I returned to Paris years later that I learned I had helped two of the most notorious lesbians in Paris escape the Germans. They were bad enough with their bickering and the mannish-looking one giving orders to the other, but what followed was even worse. On the road, we ran into an actor I knew only slightly, and his wife. They had an old, broken-down car, and were trying to get to the border. The women with me didn't want to go to the border for some reason, so the actor gave them his car and continued on with me. We traveled at night, and all day he and his wife shot cocaine. War certainly does make strange bedfellows!

"Well, what was I to do? The Germans were everywhere, in all the lands I knew. But I had friends and relatives in Argentina and that's where I went and lived until the war was over. I made two movies there, *El Viaje Sin Regreso* and the adaptation of Balzac's novel, *La Piel de Zapa*."

After the war, Florence returned to France and starred in several films. Then, she made *Krakatit*, the motion picture adaptation of Karel Capek's best-selling novel. It was the only film she ever made in her native land of Czechoslovakia. In 1949, she was summoned to the United States and starred in *Sealed Verdict* with Ray Milland and *Tokyo Joe* with Humphrey Bogart. Then she traveled to Japan to star in an American production, *Tokyo File 212*. When not working, she spent her free time entertaining the American troops in Korea.

Meanwhile, tragedy was stalking Florence Marly. She had signed to star in *El Idolo* for American producer Tom Lewis in Chile. The film had a three week shooting schedule, after which she intended to return to Hollywood to make two more films.

"It's a good thing I took my fur coat with me," she later remarked dryly. "It was four years before I was allowed to return to the United States."

Florence left for Chile at the height of the McCarthy hearings, which ignited a Hollywood purge and the infamous "blacklist."

"When I went back to renew my visa at the American Consulate in Santiago, the man in charge—a Mr. McLain—told me to come back in a week and everything would be in order. That didn't worry me because I was not due to go to work at Paramount for ten days.

"A week passed and I went back. Mr. McLain said to me, 'I could give you your visa to return to the United States, if you were fit to enter the United States.'

"I thought I had misunderstood him. I asked him to repeat what he had said.

"'You are not fit to enter the United States,' he said. 'And you will never work in Hollywood again.'

"I couldn't believe what I'd heard. I asked him why and he showed me the door. I don't know how I got back to the hotel from there. I was dazed, in a state of shock. What had I done? I pleaded with them to tell me of what I was accused, week after week, but no one at the American Consulate would take my telephone calls or even see me when I was there to plead.

"It was six months before I could even learn of what I had been accused. In the meantime, my agent was calling me from Hollywood, telling me I must return as I had films to do there. I couldn't even tell him why I wasn't able to return, because no one would tell me.

"Tom Lewis was making another film there called *Confesion al Amanecer* and I worked in that. Finally, a new man was sent to replace McLain at the Consulate, a man named Blue. I made an appointment with him. It was awful. The Americans I had learned to love turned away from me when I entered the Consulate. Mr. Blue didn't even bother to stand up when I entered his office.

"'Of what am I accused?' I asked. He pointed to a book on communism.

"I almost fainted. I had never been interested in political theories, one way or the other.

"'You think I am a communist?' I asked. He pointed to a file on his desk, a thick file, four inches high. 'This is your file,' he told me. 'We know you are.'

"It was a nightmare. I went home and carefully examined my past. I was born in Czechoslovakia which had become communist, but not for years after I left for Paris. I had made *Krakatit* after the war...but a communist! I had never even had one for a friend. My brother, who still lived in Czechoslovakia, had chosen not to join the party in spite of great pressure.

"When I made *Krakatit* in Prague, I'd left all my salary

there—almost $100,000—because friends and relatives needed it so bad. They were so poor, so sad. For that, I was being accused of being a communist, I asked myself.

"But, only a few months before, I had been cleared by the United States Security to go to Tokyo to make a film and on to Korea to entertain the soldiers. None of it made any sense.

"The months passed, and I had to sell my jewelry, my clothes, just to live. I was too ashamed to tell my friends back in Hollywood why I couldn't return.

"Again and again, I tried to get some explanation from the American Embassy, but they would never tell me exactly what I had done, or who had accused me. I was put on the blacklist and no American would speak to me. That hurt more than anything, because I had come to love America. I would meet Americans in the street and they would turn the other way. Once, I saw some people I knew and made a dinner date with them for the following evening; they didn't show up. An American film company executive told me not to come to a party his company was giving for some visiting stars. The hurts were so, so many."

Florence continued in vain to seek help from the American Consulate in Chile for nearly two years. Then, she went to Mexico, where she pleaded for another two and a half years before her name was cleared.

"There is no greater dishonor, no greater heartbreak than to be put on the blacklist by those one loves.

"I sold everything I owned. My jewels, one by one, some of them were family heirlooms [she was born a countess in her native Moravia], all the possessions I owned, and almost died of a broken heart. Some nights I would go to bed and hope that I would not awaken again. Still, I never really gave up hope. Truth is a divine substance that penetrates the thickest walls, the hardest rocks and rises above. I waited for the miracle. And I believe in miracles because one happened to me.

"To keep my sanity, I devoted my energies to humanitarian causes, the medical therapy of a wonderful man, a

Mexican doctor named Rosete. I studied. I read. And I prayed.

"Finally, a miracle happened. A new consul took over the case, a wonderful woman named Carey C. White. She gave me an appointment. That alone made me cry, because it had been years since an American official would even let me plead my case. Mrs. White listened and asked me to write down all I told her, which I did. She contacted Washington, which none of the others had even bothered to do, and learned that they had no file on me.

"All the while, I had been paying for the crimes of a Russian nightclub singer named Anna Marley. And all the while I was being kept out of the country and away from my work, Anna Marley was right here, in Los Angeles, singing at small clubs."

The case of mistaken identity and the priggishness on the part of United States Consulate officials had created a nightmare for Florence Marly, which cost her a career that promised greatness in Hollywood.

"The real tragedy of Florence," says stage actress June Wilkinson, who worked with Marly, "is it not only cost her a career, but it was so terribly unfair . . . She looked more like a movie star than any movie star I ever saw."

Upon her return to Hollywood, Florence found that people had not only all but forgotten her, but that something of a stigma still remained on her name. She had been accused, and, for many people, that was enough.

"Even after I'd been cleared and my story had been in the papers and on television, I was at a party one night and a friend started to introduce me to Jack Warner. He turned his back on me."

Unable to get work in films, Florence turned to the theater, but she was difficult to cast because of her slight accent. Then, in the 1960s, Curtis Harrington cast her in *Queen of Blood* with Dennis Hopper. Excellent reviews brought attention to Florence once again. Said *Motion Picture Daily*: "Florence Marly plays the nearly human being...picked up as a survivor from the alien space ship; a female creature with the form of a human being, a green skin, hypnotic eyes and a rather strange diet: blood...and she makes her one of the most frightening creatures in horror film history. She does so without words, just a penetrating gaze and a curling lip."

Queen of Blood became a cult film, renamed *Blood Planet* for television, and led to Florence's casting in more horror films, such as Eddie Saeta's *Dr. Death* in 1972. She also did a guest cameo appearance in Harrington's *Games*, starring Simone Signoret. But the chance for a major film career had been destroyed.

She was never bitter. "I have no time to be bitter," she said in an interview in the early 1970s. "The past is past, and people who waste time hating are poor indeed. Only mediocre people hate and I dislike mediocrity. Mediocrity and masses. That is why it was so ironic that I was accused of being a communist. Nothing bores me more than mass culture. I love individual, daring people. People with talent are the ones I admire. Talent is a precious gift and some of the human mutations are so rich in it—human mutations that would not be tolerated in a communistic society. Talent and faithfulness are the two important things in my life. I consider faithfulness a great luxury. It is a privilege to be exclusive."

A year following this interview, Florence Marly was dead. She died of a heart attack at the age of fifty-eight. Florence was still beautiful, still mysterious—and still shunned by the major motion picture producers.

Less than a hundred people attended her funeral—yet Linda Darnell had been a major star, first coming to public attention in the 1940's. She was a Cinderella girl, the flawless beauty. Her films drew millions of fans, but, by the 1960's she was all but forgotten. While visiting friends in Chicago, Linda Darnell was burned to death while sleeping on a downstairs sofa when the house caught fire.

Dallas-born Monetta Eloyse Darnell's life paralleled many a Hollywood career, encompassing beauty and an extremely ambitious mother—one who felt she could and should have been a star herself. Add the tap-dancing lessons from age five, contests of every kind from age eleven, a Hollywood screen test at sixteen and, a little later, a seven-year contract with Twentieth Century-Fox.

Linda's exotic beauty was seen in *The Mark of Zorro*, *Blood and Sand*, and *Forever Amber*. Beauty was the key word in Hollywood at the time and it was beauty that unlocked the door for Linda Darnell. The press was fond of quoting her as saying that privately she found her beauty a heavy burden.

She was much younger than her sultry looks implied when she came to Hollywood; she seldom knew how to handle the extreme attention she received from men.

Cinematographers adored her because her face photographed flawlessly from any angle. She fell in love with the man who shot her screen test and who was the cameraman on her first three movies. His name was Peverell Marley, and she went to him from the start with her problems and questions—and consequently developed an enormous crush on him. He kept discouraging her. Having been in an unhappy marriage that ended in divorce, he had a somewhat cynical view of romantic involvement. Linda tried everything to change his mind, including eloping with an actor "to show Pev." Just as the marriage ceremony was about to begin, she couldn't go through with it, broke down, confessed that she loved someone else and went home.

In 1943—she was 21 and Marley 42—they married in Las Vegas. Linda was happy and her career benefitted from Marley's knowledge and sound advice.

She landed one of the year's juiciest roles when she was given *Forever Amber*, but the movie turned out to be a costly flop—in 1947 a six million dollar film was no small thing.

Her private life was far from perfect. She and Pev had trouble; Howard Hughes paid attention to her; and she learned that she could never have children. Linda and Pev separated for over a year, but reunited and adopted a baby girl. It did not help; the marriage collapsed.

From then on, her life went on a downhill course. No earth-shattering tragedies, no tremendous failures, just unwise marriages and undemanding parts that got smaller and smaller.

At the time of her divorce, Fox cancelled her contract, and, before long, she experienced financial difficulties. She worked on physically hard films, had some health problems, and complained to the press that if she managed to get one date a month she was lucky. "My life is a king-sized vacuum, except for my daughter Lola." She told interviewers, "It would be nice to have a man around the house again."

Eating dinner alone, making decisions alone, and taking parts she did not want because she needed the money began to take its toll. She contemplated suicide, dubbing it her "night of horror," and began to realize that "my problems were not those of my real self, but a sort of synthetic, unreal self known as Linda Darnell."

After spending some time in Italy in 1954, she announced her marriage, after the fact, to Philip Liebmann of the Liebmann Breweries. She declared herself ecstatically happy.

Eighteen months later, she obtained a Mexican divorce. Four days later her husband married a younger woman.

The press began to refer to her as a "fly-by-night star," as her career stood still and she accepted parts that did not add up to much. She remarried, this time to an airline pilot, Merle Roy Robertson. After five years, in a bitter divorce, the two accused each other of unfaithfulness and drunkenness.

In 1965, Darnell was acting in small theaters around the country and arrived in Chicago, where her former secretary lived. Linda stayed with her and her family and, on the evening of April 8th, they watched *Stardust*, Linda's 1940 movie, on the late show, and had a good laugh together. Everyone went to bed late.

A few hours later, fire swept through the house. Instead of leaving the burning building, Linda went to wake up her friend's sixteen-year-old daughter. She did not realize that the young girl had already left the house with the rest of the family. Linda collapsed inside the house.

When firemen found Linda, her nightclothes were charred and over eighty percent of her body was burned. She recovered consciousness, asked about her own daughter, and then lapsed into a coma. Twenty-four hours later, the "Cinderella Girl" was dead at the age of forty-three.

"A blessing," commented one fire fighter who had seen her face.

CHAPTER 4

Sudden Exits

Was Thomas Ince shot to death on William Randolph Hearst's yacht? Was it a hushed-up murder? And, if so, was it a case of mistaken identity? And was the intended victim Charlie Chaplin, making Ince's shooting really an accident after all?

These rumors have circulated ever since November 19, 1924. Producer, director, screenwriter and sometimes actor Thomas H. Ince, then forty-two-years old, a man of keen vision and one of the most important influences during the early days of cinema, died mysteriously after a weekend aboard the controversial newspaper king's luxurious yacht, "Oneida."

The official reason for Ince's death was given as heart failure due to acute indigestion.

On the following day, *The New York Times* reported that Ince, the "maker of stars," died "early this morning from angina pectoria at his home in the Hollywood foothills. His death ended an illness that began Monday [three days earlier] while he was en route to San Diego. The suddenness of the attack prompted his friends to take him from a train at Delmar, then to hurry him to Los Angeles in a special car, during which journey he was attended by two specialists and three nurses. From Los Angeles, he was taken to his canyon home, where his wife, his two sons and two brothers rushed to his bedside before the end came."

There was no mention of the weekend on board the

yacht. Instead, it was stated that Ince died just as he was about to expand into a collaboration which would connect his film fortunes with those of William Randolph Hearst. They were at the point of concluding a deal and their first project would have been *The Enchanted Isle*.

Then, in December, *The New York Times* reported drily that there would be "no official investigation" into the death of Ince.

Meanwhile, there were whispers that the dynamic, and occasionally ruthless, Ince had been flirting with Hearst's lady, Marion Davies, and that, in a fit of jealousy, Hearst had fired a fatal shot. Another insistent rumor was that one of the other guests, none other than Charlie Chaplin, was attracted to Marion and had flirted openly with her. And there were those who insisted Charlie and Marion were having an affair which had been going on for some time.

Hearst became angry and, before anybody knew what was happening, he fired a shot from his revolver. The bullet—meant for Chaplin—happened to hit Ince.

It has also been said that Louella Parsons, one of the two queens of gossip (the other being Hedda Hopper), received her position of importance and considerable power in the Hearst newspaper syndicate because she had been present during that weekend and knew what had, in fact, happened.

The truth will never be known, for all the principals in this particular drama are long since dead. But, so far as Hollywood goes, Parsons and Hopper may have been the initiators of the idea that "I'll write whatever you want if you treat me right."

An accidental death has shook Hollywood more than once, such as the tragedy that befell Primula Rollo Niven.

The pretty British girl with the flowery name felt that she was on top of the world as 1944 drew to a close. The horrors of World War II were finally over, horrors she had experienced first-hand, having served as a WAAF officer.

She was married to a man she and the world adored, the witty, romantic actor David Niven. They had two small sons, and now the family was moving to America.

Six months after their arrival in Hollywood, the Nivens were invited to a party specifically arranged so that David's friends could meet Primula and she them. It was held at the elegant home of Tyrone Power, who was in the midst of filming his first film after the war, *The Razor's Edge*. He and his wife, French actress Annabella, kept up their tradition of "Sunday at the Powers." It meant that close friends dropped by for a swim, an early barbecue and then an evening of pure relaxation, which often meant playing charades and other games.

"Actors tend to keep their childishness," David had told Primula—whom he affectionately called Primmie. "We do really silly things. Practical jokes. Games."

It was a beautiful Sunday in May of 1945. Twenty-eight- year old Primula arrived on the arm of her husband and met his friends. Besides the host and hostess, other guests included Cesar Romero, Patricia Medina, Oleg Cassini, Gene Tierney, Rex Harrison and Lilli Palmer. They all made Primula feel totally accepted and welcome. Everybody loved David Niven and, as his wife, she was immediately included in their warmth.

The afternoon and evening added up to a definite success. Some people left after the barbecue and the smaller group moved indoors and began playing elaborate charades. Primmie had a great time and, when someone suggested they play "Sardines," she was as enthusiastic as the rest. It was a child's game. All the lights were turned off and everybody except the person who was "it" would hide. The one who managed to stay hidden to the very last was the winner.

Of course, Primmie did not know the lay-out of the house. She felt her way around, found a door, took it to be a closet of some kind and stepped quickly inside. But the door led down to the cellar. She tumbled down the steps and landed on the stone floor below.

David Niven was hiding under a bed in an upstairs room when Tyrone Power came running to tell him that Primmie had fallen down the cellar steps. She was unconscious. A doctor was called, but the fall did not seem serious. She was diagnosed as having a concussion and taken to the hospital.

Everyone waited, a bit shaken, but not really worried. David returned from the hospital and reassured them that Primmie was all right. "She'll have to stay in the hospital a few days, that's all."

The next morning, however, David was told that a blood clot had formed in his wife's brain and she had to undergo surgery immediately. An hour later, she was dead.

A brilliant young German director, F. W. Murnau, had quite an impact on the world cinema in 1922 with *Nosferatu-Eine Symphonie des Grauens*. The film was followed by another masterpiece in 1924, *Der letzte Mann*, so visually expressive that the customary film titles were unnecessary. Fox Studios invited him to Hollywood and he arrived early in 1927. His first Hollywood film, *Sunrise*, opened to raves the same year.

Murnau was haughty, arrogant, an introverted homosexual, slow to learn English—and a man whose name would have been part of American film history today had his life not ended in 1931 at the age of forty-two. He had just finished the film *Tabu* in partnership with celebrated documentary director Robert Flaherty. The movie was due to open in one week, when Murnau came back to California and decided to drive to Monterey for a few days. On a whim, he handed the wheel of his hired Packard to his young and handsome Filipino valet, who promptly ran the car off the road. The boy survived; Murnau was killed.

A plane crash took the life of rambunctious comedienne Carole Lombard, just thirty-three, while she was on a war bond drive in the early days of 1942. She and her mother were on a small plane that slammed into a mountain wall south of Las Vegas. Lombard's husband, Clark Gable—they were an intensely happy Hollywood couple—flew to the area and waited with an aching heart as the rescue team, headed by an old Indian, made the treacherous climb to the charred plane wreck. Shortly thereafter, Gable enlisted in the Army Air Corps. In 1934, before Lombard met Clark Gable, she was engaged to marry singer Russ Columbo. One day, as Russ was visiting a friend who showed him some antique guns he had bought, one of the guns accidentally discharged. The bullet penetrated the area above the singer's eye, killing him instantly.

Actor Leslie Howard was killed when a plane he was aboard was shot down by German raiders during World War II.

Ironically, Howard, fifty years old when he died, had served in World War I, been shell-shocked and recovered through therapeutic acting lessons.

The world's movie audiences remember him as Ashley Wilkes in *Gone with the Wind*, and as the leading man in *The Petrified Forest*, *Of Human Bondage*, *Pygmalion*, *The Scarlet Pimpernel* and many other films both in the United States and Great Britain.

His fateful plane trip followed a British government-sponsored lecture tour of Lisbon and cities of Spain.

Many people believe that the plane was shot down because British Prime Minister Winston Churchill was thought to be on board.

It could also have been Leslie Howard who was the real target. There were rumors that he was actually on a spy mission for his government—and certainly the German leaders were not happy about his effective propaganda work. Interestingly, the man who projected the perfect image of the WASP on screen and stage was orthodox in his Jewish faith—he would never work on the Sabbath, for instance.

These are the details that are known about his last day.

Shortly before 9:30 a.m., Tuesday, June 1, 1943, thirteen passengers boarded a camouflage-painted DC-3 at the Portela airport outside Lisbon. There were eight men, three women and two children on their way to England. The plane had a crew of four, all Dutch. The flight number was 777.

The plane never reached its destination, Whitchurch airport outside Bristol. Above the Bay of Biscay, German fighters were waiting, stationed near Bordeaux in occupied France. The DC-3 was hit by enemy fire and dove, engulfed in flames, into the sea. All seventeen aboard were killed. No bodies, nor any pieces of wreckage, have ever been found. Nobody knows why this unarmed plane was shot down.

The incident received enormous world-wide publicity because British actor Leslie Howard was among the seventeen people killed. Howard, one of the most acclaimed actors of his time, left a soaring career in 1939 to take an active part in the war against the Nazis, creating radio broadcasts whose contents made government officials gasp. He wrote angry articles for both British and American publications and he made *Pimpernel Smith*, a propaganda film about an absentminded professor who fools the Nazis. The movie became an enormous success and made people laugh at a time when there wasn't much about which to laugh.

The movie made terrific fun of the Nazis and when Leslie Howard moved on to do other propaganda films, the Germans put his name on their special black list.

In the spring of 1943, the British Council asked Howard to go on a lecture tour to Portugal and Spain. One day, toward the end of April, he landed in Lisbon. Lisbon was neutral and, at the time, a haven for spies of every nationality. It was Europe's back door to the United States. Everybody spied on everyone else.

The air traffic between England and Portugal—one plane a day in each direction—was managed with the silent permission of the Germans. It was important to the enemy, since they smuggled agents headed for England in these planes.

The KLM airline had been flying every day for three years, and brought more than 5,500 passengers to and from Lisbon without mishap. The Germans also flew to Lisbon; Lufthansa had its own building at the airport. Gestapo agents watched every plane that arrived and every plane that left. They knew the names of everyone who flew in or out of Lisbon.

The German Embassy knew the moment Leslie Howard stepped off the plane. Both German and British spies kept him under surveillance at numerous cocktail parties, press events and dinners.

Howard then continued to Madrid by train. The Germans sent forward their secret weapon, one Baroness Miranda, a dark-haired Argentine beauty who—after a failed marriage to a German nobleman—had become one of Nazi Admiral Canaris's spies. She was placed strategically at Madrid's finest hotel, where Leslie Howard stayed, and was a frequent guest at diplomatic festivities in the city.

The Germans were certain that Howard had not traveled to the Spanish capital just to speak about Hamlet. They guessed at some secret mission. Therefore, the baroness was sent to charm Howard. It seems that she may have, at least for a short time. British spies warned him about her, but perhaps the thought of romancing a German spy amused him. When he left Madrid, the baroness was at the train station, waving good-bye to him.

Was Leslie Howard a British agent? There has never been a definite answer to the question. The British officials have kept their silence.

Nor was Leslie Howard's death mentioned during the many war crime trials in Germany after the end of the war. No German documents have been found that could shed light on the matter.

Leslie Howard spent the last days of his life at the Hotel Atlantico in Estoril outside Lisbon. The Germans planted another female at that hotel too, but Howard rejected her.

Early Tuesday morning, he went to the airport. About fifty people were there to say good-bye. He was the last passenger to enter the plane.

Of all the theories about why the plane was shot down, only two seem plausible. According to the first, the target was definitely Leslie Howard because he was Jewish, because he made outrageous fun of the Nazis and because he was a suspected British agent.

The second theory is that the actual target was the prime minister of England, Winston Churchill. Documented evidence states that Hitler often toyed with thoughts of assassinating Churchill. But why would the Germans think that Churchill was in Lisbon on June 1, 1943, and that he would be careless enough to choose a plane without escorts and security for his return to London?

It so happened that Churchill had a look-alike, namely Howard's financial advisor and companion on this trip, Alfred Chenhalls. People often commented on how much he looked like Churchill, although he was younger, taller and more muscular. When he boarded the plane, possibly an eager German agent reported that Churchill had just done so.

Days before Flight 777 took off on its doomed journey, there had been rumors that Churchill was in Lisbon. Actually, he was in Algiers, but the whole world knew that he would return home shortly.

Even if it seems unlikely that Churchill would take a regular plane in full daylight, he himself believed he was the intended victim and mentioned it in the fourth part of his memoirs.

The Dutch radioman aboard the DC-3 told the control tower outside of Bristol at 12:54: "Unidentified plane is following us . . ." Seconds later, he said, "We are being shot at by unidentified airplane . . ." Then, the contact was broken.

There was still hope at the time. The plane had enough fuel to keep flying another five hours and there were two inflatable boats aboard. But hours went by and nothing more was reported. At dawn, planes were dispatched to search for survivors. It was all in vain. The search had to be abandoned because of bad weather. The Bay of Biscay had lived up to its reputation.

The world mourned a fine actor and an articulate, gentle man.

In March of 1958, Mike Todd, producer and promoter, was aboard his private plane, "The Lucky Liz," which was named after his wife of about a year, Elizabeth Taylor. He was on his way to New York where the National Association of Theater Owners was honoring him as "Showman of the Year." The plane crashed, killing all those aboard. Elizabeth Taylor had intended to make the journey with him, but a sudden, severe cold prevented her from doing so. Todd left a legacy of the spectacular success of *Around the World in Eighty Days* and *Oklahoma* as well as the memory of a man who was tremendously alive and passionately in love with show business. David Niven said about him, "Todd's the best thing that's happened to Hollywood. I'm so sick of dreary bankers that call themselves producers. He's a man with vision and some guts and generosity." Yes, indeed, Mike Todd was a showman.

A small charter flight from Atlanta crashed in the wooded mountain area northwest of Roanoke, Virginia. The wreckage and the bodies of Audie Murphy, age forty-six, and five others were not found for three days.

So ended the life of the most decorated American war hero of World War II. Murphy, the son of poverty-stricken Texas cotton sharecroppers, was awarded twenty-four decorations, including the Congressional Medal of Honor. His face appeared on the cover of *Life* magazine and Hollywood took note of his boyish handsomeness. He starred in several westerns and played himself in *To Hell and Back*, which was based on the book about his life.

A simple, sweet man, who was eager to share his good luck with others, Murphy shrugged when people praised his bravery during the war. "My family was poor. Even as a small boy, if I was to shoot a hare for dinner, I wasn't allowed to waste more than one shot. War was hell—but I hadn't much to look forward to after it. Bravery often means that you don't have much to lose."

He survived the war, but was plagued by nightmares and jumpiness. "I can sit at a bar and somebody slams the door—my reflexes go into action and I am ready to kill. Have you thought of how they re-train dogs after a war, but not the men?"

In 1970, he was cleared of attempted murder charges after beating up a man in a barroom brawl.

Audie Murphy's life became complex after the war. He was a boy who killed 240 Germans and then became a movie star; a guy who loved his two sons, but wished almost desperately for a daughter; and a man who died tragically in a plane crash at a time when he was attempting to put his life into order, revive his fading career and straighten out his tangled finances.

Ricky Nelson began his career at the age of twelve, playing himself in "The Adventures of Ozzie and Harriet," a show that lasted fourteen years on ABC. Witty and confident from the beginning, Ricky was a rebellious boy and a contrast to his older brother, David, who seemed to have accepted the fact that he was just the fourth member of a phenomenally successful television show that ultimately had little to do with him. Ricky branched out to adult roles, such as in the John Wayne western *Rio Bravo* when he was just eighteen, and then entered the music scene. He married and dropped the "y" from his name. However, real stardom escaped him and he spent the last twenty years of his life trying to tap into the success of his earlier life. The peaks of his career had happened too early—nothing later matched them. In the 1980s, he toured the country, nearly forgotten, performing at fairs and restaurants. His marriage was a bitter memory, and his worries about losing his looks reached the point where he refused to leave his house without putting on makeup.

The witty, beloved boy, who was a millionaire before his twenty-first birthday, died in an airplane crash on December 21, 1985 near De Kalb, Texas. Rick Nelson was forty-four years old—a troubled, reclusive man, who was a million dollars in debt.

For weeks, the tabloids featured stories about the accident that took the life of Princess Grace of Monaco—or Grace Kelly, as moviegoers still thought of her. The actress, who gave up her career to become a real-life princess, zealously guarded her private life. She would have hated the speculations about that fateful day in 1982 when a Rover sedan in which she and her teenage daughter Stephanie were driving veered off a steep mountain road and crashed. Stephanie survived—Grace Kelly did not.

Grace Kelly had a charmed life for fifty-two years, during which time the media treated her well. But the vulture instincts in the press awakened after her death, wishing to tear the gossamer veils apart to "reveal" anything bordering upon the sordid.

William Holden was alone in his apartment in Santa Monica, California, on that November night in 1981. He fell against a bedside table, drunk, and bled to death from a gash in his forehead.

"He had his devils," said Blake Edwards, who directed Holden's final movie, *S.O.B.*

"He was that rare creature—a beautiful American, " said Billy Wilder.

Holden was a complex man, alternately called gregarious and introspective, physical and intellectual. In the late 1950s, he used the riches he reaped from movies like *The Bridge on the River Kwai* to flee from Hollywood.

Travel was his passion. He established an African wildlife resort in Kenya and was deeply committed to animal preservation. He spent much time in Hong Kong and Japan, since he had business interests there. He also collected tribal art from New Guinea.

All during his life, Holden said that he owed his career to the support of Barbara Stanwyck. An established star, she was cast in the lead opposite Holden in *The Golden Boy*. The director did not like the young and inexperienced actor and kept threatening to fire him. Becoming tired of these threats, Stanwyck issued an ultimatum to the director: "If Bill goes, I go." For the rest of his life, Holden sent Stanwyck a large bouquet of yellow sweetheart roses on her birthday.

In 1947, Swedish-born Marta Toren was discovered by Hollywood and was quickly dubbed, "The Eyes." She had unusual, almond-shaped, blue-grey eyes, made intense by the Technicolor camera. She appeared in *Casbah* and ten other movies, but did not like Hollywood at all, claiming it was "not inducive to real work." She left for Europe and made movies in Italy and Spain. Ten years later, at age thirty, Marta Toren died suddenly from a brain hemorrhage.

The zany antics of cigar-chomping comic Ernie Kovacs rocketed him to stardom. The man who created a brand of humor that was unique—and influenced television forever—was killed shortly before two a.m. on January 13, 1962, when his station wagon skidded across wet pavement and smashed into a power pole in West Los Angeles.

Kovacs and his wife, actress Edie Adams, had attended a baby shower and left the party in separate cars for the ten-minute drive from the house of their host, director Billy Wilder, to their seventeen-room mansion.

Edie Adams reached home—totally unaware of the crash.

The movie camera was rolling as Tyrone Power and

George Sanders were filming a sword fight. *Solomon and Sheba* was shot in Madrid, and the two played brothers fighting to the death to determine who would rule Israel. Both men were clad in heavy robes and handled the fifteen pound swords with the skill of seasoned movie heroes. Numerous takes were ordered.

After the eighth take, the normally patient and accommodating Power threw down his sword. "I have had it," he remarked. He was shaking and complained that he felt cold. There was no doctor on the set, but Power's makeup man, who had been with him for years, sensed that the star was seriously ill. Power was taken to the nearest hospital, but emergency procedures were useless. Power was dead-on-arrival. He was forty-four-years old.

The man who was an enigma to many, one of the most gorgeous men ever to illuminate the movie screen, had reached the final reel of his life.

Who was Tyrone Power? His unusually good looks—Power's long, thick eyelashes actually threw shadows on his cheeks—were a burden to the man whose intense ambition was to become a good actor rather than a movie star. Power had a delicate, masculine beauty and possessed a marvelous speaking voice. The son and grandson of actors, Power was married three times—to French actress Annabella, to actress Linda Christian and to Debbie Minardos—and was known to have had love affairs with Judy Garland, Lana Turner and Anita Ekberg. He fathered two daughters, Romina and Taryn, by Linda Christian, and a son, Tyrone Power IV, was born to Debbie two months after his death. He was a man of class, manners and a quick mind. During the second World War, he joined the Marine Corps and logged eleven hundred hours of flying time, much of it under enemy fire.

Power was a very private man and was the main male star at 20th Century-Fox from the late 1930s until the war.

His funeral became a circus, with invited mourners having to fight their way through throngs of fans. Many had brought small children and picnic lunches. His widow had forbidden Linda Christian to attend the funeral, so, a few hours later, Linda and Power's two daughters arrived alone and placed a large cross of white gardenias on his grave.

Among those paying their last respects were Henry Fonda, James Stewart, Gregory Peck, Billy Wilder, Danny Kaye, Clifton Webb, Robert Wagner, Natalie Wood and Loretta Young. Yul Brynner, who replaced Tyrone Power in *Solomon and Sheba*, also attended. Fans applauded the stars enthusiastically, while others sobbed and screamed, "Tyrone, we love you."

March 25, 1982, was a day when life changed for several people in Hollywood. That was the day when John Belushi was found dead from an overdose of cocaine and heroin. Fans were shook by the news—as were several actor friends—to the point that they took a hard look at their own cocaine habits.

"John was indestructible," said a friend. "If he couldn't take it, who can?"

The star of "Saturday Night Live" and *Animal House* had sped down the fast line. John was dead at the age of thirty-three.

Jamaican-born actor/director/producer Frank Silvera would have turned fifty-six the following month, but died on June 12, 1970. He was electrocuted while repairing a garbage disposal unit in the kitchen of his Pasadena home. Audiences remember him most vividly as "General Huerta" in Elia Kazan's *Viva Zapata* and as the Mexican ranch owner on the television series "High Chaparral."

He wanted immortality and he got it. Even after his death, he was the most popular actor in Hollywood, receiving up to eight thousand fan letters monthly.

He is a prime example of a legend that grew into almost macabre proportions.

Many refused to believe what happened on September 30, 1955, when James Byron Dean sped his silver Porshe Spyder, which he bought only days earlier, through the intersection of California routes 466 and 41, a mile east of Cholame, as he was on his way to Salinas to compete in a racing event. A life of a mere twenty-four years came to an abrupt end. In only three starring roles—*Rebel Without a Cause, Giant*, and *East of Eden* (the only film movie audiences had seen at the time)—he had established himself as a symbol of a whole "live fast, die young" generation. Later generations have picked up on the still thriving James Dean cult.

The day before the crash in which he died, he had wrapped *Giant*, in which he starred with Elizabeth Taylor and Rock Hudson. Ironically, during the filming of the movie, he appeared in a commercial for safe driving: "Take it easy—the life you save may be mine . . ." Dean was in a mood of celebration as he drove north, laughing and talking with his companion, a stuntman. Earlier in the afternoon, he had gotten a speeding ticket outside of Bakersfield. About 5:30 in the afternoon, another car appeared from the intersection, turning left onto the highway. In the beginning twilight, the Porshe may have blended with the sky, reflecting the last rays of the sun. The two cars collided. The left side of Dean's car crumpled. He died almost instantly while his passenger was thrown from the car with serious injuries. The driver of the other car, a college student, had only minor injuries.

Born in Marion, Indiana, on February 8, 1931, the son of a dental technician, Dean's family moved to Los Angeles when he was five. After his mother's death when he was eight, he returned to the Midwest and was raised on a relative's farm in Iowa. After graduating from high school, Dean returned to California, where he attended Santa Monica Junior College and the University of California in Los Angeles. He began acting with James Whitmore's theater group, appeared in occasional television commercials, and did bits in a few movies. In 1952, he went to New York, where he earned his living as a busboy. Finally, he

landed a part in *See The Jaguar* on Broadway. He studied
acting at Actors Studio (or at least attended classes as an
observer) and won attention in the Broadway play *The
Immoralist* in 1954. This led to a screen test with Warner
Brothers and a remarkable—though brief—movie career.

As an amateur race driver, a wild and possibly, at
times, kinky party-participant, and rebellious and sensitive
personality on the movie screen, Dean seemed to person-
ify the restless American youth of the mid-50s.

At his funeral in Fairmount, Indiana, the eulogy delivered by the Reverend Harvey ended with, "The career of
James Dean has not ended. It has just begun. And remember, God himself is directing the production."

The reverend probably did not mean it the way events
have turned out—with hordes of fans stubbornly insisting
that Dean is in hiding, terribly disfigured.

Some people have made a lot of money out of the
tragedy, including selling alleged pieces of the Porsche in
which Dean died. Stone sculptures of Dean's head were
sold, and one company even marketed a life-size head
shaped by something they called Miracleflesh, a soft plastic
material that looked and felt like human flesh.

The world had not seen its like since the days in the
1920s, when the Valentino cult raged.

Later, the usual rumors and stories surfaced. The
popular question in the '90s seems to focus on a dead star's
sex life: was he or she gay or straight? When the rumors
about James Dean grew, Dennis Hooper spoke out in
Mirabella, saying, "James Dean was not gay. The two great
loves of his life were Pier Angeli and Ursula Andress. Pier
married Vic Damone. Jimmy sat in the rain on his motorcycle outside the church. She'd asked Jimmy to marry her.
He asked her to wait until he saw how his career was going. Ursula Andress married John Derek and proceeded to
parade him onto the set of *Giant* after Jimmy refused to
marry her for the same reason."

James Dean's costar in *Rebel Without a Cause* was a
lovely teenager named Natalie Wood. Her untimely death

in 1981—she was forty-three years old—was another shock that reverberated through Hollywood and the world. She, her husband Robert Wagner, and actor Christopher Walken were aboard the Wagners' yacht at Santa Catalina Island's Isthmus Cove. During the night, the petite, dark-eyed actress apparently slipped and fell into the water. She drowned without anyone hearing or noticing anything.

Natalie Wood was born Natasha Gurdin on July 20, 1938, in San Francisco, California. The daughter of an architect of Russian extraction and a ballet dancer of French descent, she took dance lessons from the age of three. At four, she made her movie debut in *Happy Land* and the director remembered her three years later when he made *Tomorrow Is Forever* with Orson Welles and Claudette Colbert. She continued working as a child star and made an unusually smooth transition into teen-age and then leading lady roles. By the time she was twenty-one years old, she had made thirty-four motion pictures.

Then, suddenly, she was hailed as a new Elizabeth Taylor. Gone was the image of the perennially mixed-up kid, with little talent for anything except being written up in fan magazines in connection with male stars. Nicky Hilton, James Dean and Elvis Presley were just a few with whom her name was linked. When she married Robert Wagner in 1957, everything looked perfect on the glossy fan magazine pages. But the marriage fell apart in 1961.

"Not to become blinded by your own glitter," she said, somewhat wistfully in the early '60s. Some, including Elia Kazan, who directed her in *Splendor in the Grass*, worried that she would not be able to survive Hollywood. She forever after credited Kazan with being the one person who started her on the road to becoming a "real actress."

"To be a woman and an actress is hard. Very hard," she said in many interviews. "My life for years was a drowning experience," she said, a seemingly prophetic choice of words.

At the time of her death, the quick and sensitive actress's life had come together. She worked hard, found increased satisfaction in her roles, lived well, enjoyed her children, threw great parties, stayed up late and loved to go sailing. Remarried to Wagner, she said happily, "R.J. and I have the same rhythm." Both were ecology-minded and health-minded. They had many friends.

Speculation followed the tragedy, but the facts point to her death being an accident. For whatever reason, Natalie seems to have put the dingy in the water and fallen in. Her fur-lined jacket became waterlogged and pulled her down.

Robert Wagner had trouble speaking her name for some time afterward.

MARY MILES MINTER

Her screen image as a proper and virginal teen-ager was ruined when director William Desmond Taylor, with whom she was romantically involved, was murdered.

DOUGLAS FAIRBANKS, MARY PICKFORD, CHARLIE CHAPLIN, D.W. GRIFFITH

Hollywood royalty, and the founders of United Artists. But Mary's brother Jack suffered from alcohol and drug abuse, and The Little Tramp was involved in a paternity scandal.

BARBARA STANWYCK
"Missy" was protected from the press by her longtime friend
and agent, Helen Ferguson.

HEDY LAMARR
Even being a major star didn't give Lamarr immunity from the print media; she was considered fair game.

TALLULAH BANKHEAD
Southern beauty, and an outspoken, lusty demeanor caught Hollowood off guard, but Tallulah's first love was the New York stage.

ROCK HUDSON

His adoring public did not know he was gay until AIDS claimed his life; Hudson acknowledged his homosexuality before he died.

GEORGE NADER
    His career took a tail spin when Universal traded *Confidential* a story on his sexuality rather than Rock Hudson's.

FATTY ARBUCKLE
Even though he was acquitted of the rape of a Hollywood starlet, the public condemned him and his career was destroyed.

MARY NOLAN
Women hated her blatant flirtatious nature; "the white flame" turned to religion and died in obscurity.

BARBARA LA MARR

She was the Elizabeth Taylor of her day, "the girl who is too beautiful," but drugs and alcohol claimed her life when she was only twenty-six.

MARIE PREVOST

Obesity killed her career, so she stopped eating and starved herself to death in 1937 at age thirty-eight.

WALLACE REID
He was the most handsome man alive and matinee idol supreme in 1919. Then morphine addiction led to death in a sanitarium padded cell.

CLARA BOW
She immortalized the "It" girl of the flapper era, married Rex Bell, and was plagued by depression and insomnia.

JOHN GILBERT
His face was his fortune; his voice was his downfall.

D.W. GRIFFITH
The creator of *Birth of a Nation* became a tragic figure in his old age, reliving the past in alcohol.

CARMEN MIRANDA

The lady with the tutti-frutti headgear added a "Souse" American flavor to many popular musical films during the '40s, such as *Doll Face*, pictured here.

FLORENCE MARLY

A case of mistaken identity got her blacklisted during the McCarthy communist witch hunt era; she missed a decade of work, and then hardly anyone cared.

LINDA DARNELL

The movie camera had a love affair with her flawless beauty. Linda tragically died in a fire, trying to save a young girl's life.

Linda Darnell

LESLIE HOWARD

Hollywood's perfect gentleman was killed when his plane was shot down during World War II, while he was working for the British war effort.

GEORGE SANDERS

The suave, world-weary personification of sophistication committed suicide as he said he would when he reached age sixty-five. Zsa Zsa Gabor was an adoring wife.

JAMES DEAN

A legend after only three movies, Jimmy's memory shines as brightly today, nearly forty years after his death.

NATALIE WOOD
Child star, teen star, adult star—her phobia of water held the morbid prophecy of her death.

Bella Darvi

BELLA DARVI
The namesake of Darryl and Virginia Zanuck took her own life after a brief moment of fame.

JEAN SEBERG
The pressure of being relentlessly hounded by the FBI proved to be the catalyst to make Jean Seberg commit suicide in Paris in 1979.

CHAPTER 5

By Their Own Hand

Why is Hollywood the place of suicides, obsessions of various kind, and outrageous behavior?

One early star said, "The fans don't really like us; they like the idea of us." Montgomery Clift put it this way, "The problem is how to remain thin-skinned and yet survive."

In his book, *The Politics of Experience*, psychologist R.D. Laing describes an individual who "cannot make a move, or make no move, without being beset by contradictory and paradoxical pressures and demands, pushes and pulls, both internally from himself, and externally from those around him. He is, as it were, in a position of checkmate."

Although Laing was writing about the experience and behavior that is termed schizophrenic, it actually describes the position of many of the screen's stars, especially in days gone by.

There existed a whole discipline of incompatible pressures, which gave fame but demanded obedience. The star had to be unique, but must conform. The old studio system was so harsh that some called it a form of slavery. Those it did not destroy were preserved by it. Joan Crawford was critical: "You manufacture toys, you don't manufacture stars." Bette Davis not only survived, but seemed to have thrived on the demands. The battle shaped her, the tremendous will power kept her going.

The "talkies" increased the chronic insecurity. From 1929, there was a great influx of fortune tellers, palmists, astrologers, and crystal gazers. Interestingly, their predictions often spanned seven years, which happened to be the period that came to be established as the term of a star's contract.

Many of the stars were high-strung, and some movie moguls preferred it that way. D.W. Griffith declared, "I prefer the young woman who has to support herself and possibly her mother. Of necessity she will work hard. Again, I prefer the nervous type. I never engage a newcomer who applies for work without showing at least a sign or two of nervousness. If she is calm, she has no imagination."

The mothers are worthy of considerable, if not always honorable, mention. The mothers of Geraldine Farrar, Clara Kimball Young, Pauline Frederick, Priscilla Dean, Lillian and Dorothy Gish were ruthlessly prompting their daughters' careers. But Mrs. Pickford was the most formidable of all.

Charlotte Pickford, the mother of Mary, took obsessive interest in every detail of her daughter's career, not the least those that dealt with money. By 1917, she had seen to it that Mary Pickford received $350,000 per picture. Mother Pickford got a $50,000 bonus and immediately offered up her son, Jack, who was to become a second-magnitude star, plagued by drug problems. He declined going with the same company (First National) for $85,000 per picture, since he preferred Sam Goldwyn.

Because of Mrs. Pickford, it was said that it "often took longer to make Mary's contract than to make her pictures."

Many of the early stars grew up without a father. Mary Pickford's dad was killed in an accident when she was four; Mae Marsh's father also died when she was four; the father of Lillian and Dorothy Gish deserted the family when they were four or five; Blanche Sweet's father disappeared when she was one and so on . . . into Marilyn Monroe and modern times.

Has Hollywood changed?

Bette Davis did not mince words. "All this nostalgia about the golden age of Hollywood is almost laughable. Hollywood hasn't changed in ways that count. No matter how we romanticize them, the golden years were hard work, as they are today. The fight is still between the artists and the money men."

Cary Grant developed his famous "Hollywood streetcar" theory about stardom. He took it from a Charlie Chaplin comedy he had seen in his youth where Chaplin boarded a trolley at the rear, moved forward, only to get kicked off at the front by the crush of all the passengers who got aboard after him. He ran back, jumped on again at the rear, holding on for dear life.

Grace Kelly said, "I hated Hollywood. It's a town without pity. I know of no other place in the world where so many people suffer from nervous breakdowns, where there are so many alcoholics, neurotics, and so much unhappiness."

Clark Gable was a man of few words. "I dreaded coming out here and it turned out like I thought it would... it stinks."

Vivien Leigh called Hollywood "a cultural desert" and Marlon Brando once likened the town to "one big cash register."

Yet the dark goddess Fame kept having that special allure. When clasped to her bosom, it seemed the glory would never stop. It may be worse to have had it and lose it, than never to have tasted the excess of fame.

The "Hollywood sign" that symbolizes the whole town to many people—sometimes the letters become crooked and a committee is formed to restore them—brings to mind Peg Entwistle and her spectacular suicide.

Peg was born in England, came to New York, and made her Broadway debut in a 1925 production of *Hamlet* at the age of seventeen. For about five years, she had great success on the New York stage and then, suddenly, her luck ran out.

Peg went to Hollywood in 1932 to try to recapture the

sweet smell of success. She got a bit part in *Thirteen Women*, but the studio did not pick up her contract option. Peg, twenty-four, could not cope with suddenly not being wanted. She climbed to the top of the Hollywood sign, which at that time read HOLLYWOODLAND—and jumped to her death from the thirteenth letter.

The following story could well be filed under "H"—Hollywood, Hollister and Hopelessness.

"I'd never do it! And if I ever were to do something so stupid as to take my own life, I'd let this whole heartless city know it!"

So spoke a beautiful girl named Susan Hollister when she heard about the death of starlet Mary Lugo. Susan knew Mary and had been seeing her quite often when she visited the Hollywood Studio Club.

The Club, a large, old California-style, white house, was built by Mary Pickford in the heart of Hollywood. Young girls from out-of-town, who came with recommendations, preferably from someone at a motion picture company, could get a simple, but clean, room and nutritious food, all for a moderate price.

A few of the girls made it. Most did not. Some returned home and found other means of satisfaction in their lives. For others, the end of the dream meant the end of life.

Mary Lugo, one of the prettiest in Hollywood's hungry young set, took a fatal dose of Seconal. Once known as New York's most beautiful showgirl, she came to Hollywood for bigger triumphs. They did not happen and she chose death. If there had not been a few receipts from a pawnshop at the scene, no one would have known the identity of this lifeless girl.

Susan Hollister knew other girls who had been unable to continue the fight: Alice Pemberton shot herself in a neighbor's garage the night her last dress was ruined, that trivial event which made her realize that she would never make it; Kitty Colman who opened the gas in her room and fell asleep forever.

Of course, Susan Hollister felt that her life would be different. She took drama classes, paid for by her parents in Denver, and she fully expected her first year in town to be a meager one. When the second year showed no more results than the first, she felt a growing desperation.

All her life, Susan had heard people say that she was "uncommonly pretty" and "ought to be in pictures." Faced with the reality in Hollywood, she was ready to give up several times. Then some tiny bit of work would come her way and rekindled her hopes.

After two years, she actually got a small part in a movie. Her parents came from Denver for the premiere. They and Susan held their breaths throughout the picture, but there was not even a moment's glimpse of Susan. Her part had ended up on the cutting room floor.

Susan shared an apartment with Lilian Alton, a girl whose life was quite similar to Susan's until she became an expert—at screaming. This kept her busy. She screamed for Paramount; she screamed for Warner Brothers; and she made a good living screaming.

Susan did not share that talent.

One day, she decided to bleach her dark hair blonde to see if that would make a difference. The following day Lilian came home from a studio where she had shown Susan's picture and managed to set up an appointment for her.

Susan went to see the producer.

"I thought you had dark hair."

"I did. Now, I'm a blonde," Susan said.

"Well, you still have brown eyes, so I can use you. It'll be four, five days work. And a couple of lines."

The film was set in Morocco. Susan was costumed in a long, hooded djellabah, complete with a veil so that only her dark eyes could be seen.

Hope welled up with this tiny break, but weeks rolled by and nothing further happened. Then, on a rainy, depressing day, her former agent called to ask her to accompany him to the Academy Awards presentation.

When he picked her up in his white Continental and handed her a white, mink coat, he told her that he wanted his girlfriends, and especially his clients, to look successful.

That night, she sat next to James Cagney and his wife. She shook hands with David Niven. She danced at the post-awards party, staring at Cary Grant, who danced right next to her. When she went to the ladies' room, Doris Day was washing her hands.

It was raining when she was driven home. At her apartment building, the two said good night and Susan gave back the fur coat. The agent drove off.

The next day the news spread, "Actors' agent murdered in his automobile."

The man had been shot in the front seat of his Continental with a .25 caliber Browning. A witness had seen a young, blonde woman in a white mink coat running away from the car.

Two detectives rang Susan's door bell. Well-known stars had testified that she had been seen with the agent the previous night, dressed in a white mink coat. She found herself the prime suspect in a murder case.

Susan Hollister got her pictures in the newspapers.

However, after three days and two nights, she was cleared and released. But Susan was in shock. She was approached by strangers on the street. Her telephone kept ringing. She was offered a part in a pornographic movie. She was confused and depressed. The years had worn her down.

Her parents pleaded with her to come home.

One day, she climbed the Hollywood hill to the world's largest illuminated sign. Susan Hollister jumped to her death from the three-story high letter "H"—her own initial—and that of Hollywood, horror and heartlessness.

In Hollywood, suicide has become an easily available door to escape the realities of lost dreams. Inexperienced girls, filled with the dreams of youth, flock to the city which holds out a promise of fulfillment. Some find the promises empty earlier in their search—and die young—while others have a brief moment of success, only to find themselves in later life alone and empty—and die old, some by their own hand and others from the sheer emptiness of their existences.

Olive Borden was an extravagant star in the silent era, but could not adjust to life away from the lights. She was one of Mack Sennett's Bathing Beauties and, later, Tom Mix's leading lady, but her career faded rapidly with the entrance of sound. Olive ended up on Skid Row in Los Angeles, a mumbling, bitter alcoholic. She died in 1947 in a hotel for destitute women.

Dorothy Comingore would have walked off with most of the votes in any 1941 "Most Likely to Succeed" poll. She appeared in Columbia comedy shorts and played leads in a couple of low-budget westerns before getting her big break in *Citizen Kane* as Kane's pathetic protégé and second wife Susan. But, after that, she was seen only in a few minor roles in movies such as *The Hairy Ape*, *Any Number Can Play* and *The Big Night*. Despair took hold of Dorothy Comingore and she ended up a prostitute. When, in 1971, she could no longer bear the sordidness, she took her own life. Her death was hardly noted; she had long been forgotten.

Then there was Phyllis Haver, who, in 1960, surrounded by glamourous shots of herself, died of barbiturate poisoning. The statuesque blonde had a successful career in about forty silent pictures, tasted fame and fortune, and married a millionaire, but, in later life, could not face the fact that she was unwanted and forgotten by a fast-moving world.

Florence Lawrence would have understood. She starred in D.W. Griffith's earliest productions and was known as "The Biograph Girl," then became "The Imp Girl," when Carl Laemmle lured her to his company. Florence was a popular movie star until the mid-20s, but then was quickly forgotten by a fickle public. She worked as an extra occasionally, but, in 1938, at fifty-two, she committed suicide by eating ant paste.

Olive Thomas escaped poverty and a teen-age marriage by going to New York, where she won a contest as "The Perfect Model." Instantly famous, she became the toast of Broadway, starring in *The Ziegfeld Follies* of 1915. Olive signed a film contract, made seventeen films, and married film actor Jack Pickford, Mary's brother.

She seemingly had an enchanted life. Yet, on September 10, 1920, a Paris hotel valet found Olive's sable coat on the floor and, lying on top of it, Olive's nude body, with a bottle of bichloride of mercury in her hand.

Why would she kill herself? The press rumored that Olive had been trying to buy large amounts of heroin for her hopelessly addicted husband—and had failed to do so.

Lupe Velez was as fiery and volatile off screen as on. She was discovered by Hal Roach and played a woman with a flaming temperament in many films. During the 1940s, she starred with comic Leon Errol in the *Mexican Spitfire* series.

She had a tempestuous three-year affair with Gary Cooper, which began when they made *Wolf Song* together. Cooper loved her, but did not want to marry her. She had other romances after Cooper and married Johnny Weissmuller—known to moviegoers from the *Tarzan* series—in 1933. Five years of public quarrels, tears, and other passionate outbursts ensued. Two divorce petitions were filed and withdrawn. "I love to fight," she told friends. When she and Johnny finally divorced, she continued to fall in love. Her affairs were always "forever and ever" and, each time, she was "ready to die" when the romance ended.

She did die by her own hand at the end of a love affair with young actor Harold Ramond. After having her hair and makeup done, she took a fatal overdose of sleeping pills. She was pregnant.

In her suicide note, she wrote:

"May God forgive you and forgive me, too. But I prefer to take my life away and our baby's before I bring him shame . . . how could you, Harold, fake such a great love for me and our baby when all the time you didn't want us? I see no other way out for me, so good-bye and good luck to you. Love, Lupe."

Ramond, an Austrian, had not been in Hollywood very long and claimed afterwards that Lupe misunderstood what he had said. When he had talked about "faking a marriage," he had meant faking the actual date to make it seem they had married earlier, before the baby was conceived. When he suggested this, Lupe had stormed out, insisting that she was not pregnant at all.

Lupe's body was found by her maid, Juanita, at Casa Felicias on North Rodeo Drive—not artfully arranged on her white bed, but in the bathroom, her silver lame gown splattered with vomit and her head stuck in the toilet bowl. The sleeping pills she took had made her violently ill and Lupe had staggered to the bathroom for relief and had drowned.

Carole Landis was a Hollywood beauty who did not make it past the age of twenty-nine. The Wisconsin blonde married a writer, twenty years her senior, before she was sixteen, but did not find security. After a variety of odd jobs, she saved up for a bus ticket to San Francisco, became a singer/hula dancer, and landed in Hollywood at the age of eighteen, pretty and, according to wide-spread opinion, with the best legs in town.

Three more marriages followed in rapid succession. During this time, she made quite a few movies and engaged in a number of liaisons. She was a girl possessed by a lust for acclaim, glamour and passion.

In 1947, at the end of her fourth marriage, she met the devastatingly charming actor Rex Harrison, who was then married to actress Lilli Palmer. Gossip columns hinted at an affair with veiled references to "a British star whose name begins with H and the local queen of glamour (her name begins with L)." Finally, Rex Harrison confessed the affair to his wife.

Two weeks after Lilli left for the East Coast, Harrison found Carole in her apartment on Capri Drive in Pacific Palisades, dressed in a dirndl dress and gold sandals, lying dead in the bathroom. A note was addressed to her mother:

"Dearest Mommie: I'm sorry, really sorry, to put you through this. But there is no way to avoid it. I love you, darling. You have been the most wonderful mom ever and that applies to all our family. I love each and every one of you dearly. Everything goes to you. Look in the files and there is a will which decrees everything. Good-by, my angel. Pray for me. Your Baby."

Her death was caused by an overdose of sleeping pills, downed with whiskey. Insistent rumors maintained that there had been a second note as well.

After notifying the authorities, Harrison called his wife, who immediately flew back to stand by his side. He met considerable hostility from the press and public alike. Twentieth Century-Fox cautiously postponed the release of his latest film, *Unfaithfully Yours*, in which he played a jealous husband plotting to kill his wife.

Carole's best friend, Dick Haymes's mother, told Harrison that Carole had made several earlier suicide attempts, but had been careful to make sure she would be rescued before it was too late. This time her behavior followed the same pattern. She made several calls and left messages with a number of friends. But on this Fourth of July holiday, people were away and did not pick up their messages. Maids had the day off. Nobody received the message in time to save Carole.

A number of stars attended her funeral at Forest Lawn Cemetery. Rex Harrison and Lilli Palmer were both staring straight ahead, expecting anything, even tangible hostility, from the crowd. Nothing happened, and Carole Landis was laid to rest.

Stardom never brought Pier Angeli happiness. The

Italian-born twin sister of Marisa Pavan first appeared in Fred Zinnemann's *Teresa* in 1951. She was brought to Hollywood as part of Metro-Goldwyn-Mayer's attempt to meet the demands of the new international cinema. In her movie debut, the critics called her "the demure Italian beauty with a luminous sensitivity."

Pier continued playing frail heroines in a number of movies and became best friends with Debbie Reynolds, who taught her American slang, and dated James Dean and Kirk Douglas. On November 24, 1954, she wed singing star Vic Damone.

Talented and sensitive—but believing strongly she was not to be fate's favorite—Pier had a troubled private life. One bright point of light was the birth of her son Perry (named after Perry Como) in spite of suffering a broken pelvis in a fall during her pregnancy. Professionally, she met with success, playing Paul Newman's wife in *Somebody Up There Likes Me*, and critics and public alike demonstrated that they did indeed like her a lot.

Her marriage had more than the usual ups and downs, separations and reconciliations. Finally, in 1957, the couple separated.

The whole idea of stardom, Hollywood style, troubled Pier deeply. Yet, she had difficulty living without it, as well. She decided to return to Europe where she appeared in a number of rather unremarkable films, except perhaps *Merry Andrew* with Danny Kaye.

After the divorce in 1959, she and Damone spent six years in court battles over their son, while she kept acting. Pier also recorded an album of Italian songs, which revealed a surprisingly rich, warm voice. She started seeing Damone again after the divorce although she married Italian bandleader Armando Trovajoli in London in 1962. However, they separated shortly after the wedding, and their son, called "Popino," was born in 1963.

In 1964, she told the press that she was lonely and felt forgotten, adding, "I am still in love, deeply and eternally, with James Dean." Friends worried about her increasing bouts with depression. In 1971, she told a journalist that she was "practically penniless. I can't go on like this." On September 10, 1971, not knowing that she had just been cast in a meaty guest-starring role on the television series "Bonanza," Pier Angeli died from an overdose of barbitu- ates. She was thirty-nine years old.

The girl who started out on a career filled with unique promise ended up deeply unhappy, feeling that she was wearing "a lying mask" and working mainly in explotation pictures. Her last movie, which was released after her death, was *Octaman*, a monster-suspense film with Jeff Morrow and Kerwin Matthews.

Capucine, another international film beauty, ended her life on March 17, 1990. The former Paris fashion model was originally discovered by designer Givenchy and then by Hollywood agent Charles Feldman, who inter- rupted a dinner with John Wayne to offer her a screen test and who remained close to her until her death.

The woman, about whom George Cukor said "the camera has a love affair with her face," jumped to her death from her eighth-floor apartment in Lausanne, Switzerland, where she lived alone with her three cats.

Born in Toulon, Capucine appeared in such films as *Song Without End*, *The Pink Panther*, and *What's New, Pussy Cat?* Her best role, however, was in *Walk on the Wild Side*, in which she played the reluctant lesbian lover to Barbara Stanwyck's vice queen. Some of the highly charged scenes between them are among Capucine's best work. Stanwyck considered the film to be among her best as well.

"My friends hated the film, or were embarrassed by it, because of the lesbian theme. When it came out, I knew they'd all rushed out to see it, but pretended they hadn't," Stanwyck said in an interview. "It was as if they were em- barrassed for me. Hell, I was proud of my work in that film and thought it was some of the best work I ever did.

"Some years later, a friend, Ray Locke, the writer, told

me that he loved the film, but thought it was made about ten or so years before the audiences were ready for that sort of story on film, or the candid treatment of the relationship between Hallie and Connie. Perhaps that was a problem. I liked it and I loved working with Capucine.

"She was lovely, wonderful to work with. Those were difficult roles for both of us and we discussed that before shooting began. There is a scene where I slap her around and I accidentally hit her rather hard on the first take. Surprise and a flash of anger crossed her face, but it was a print take and it worked beautifully.

"Later, when she saw it, she thanked me for hitting her so hard, because her surprised reaction was exactly what Hallie would have done under the circumstances. Hallie was a lady, a very beautiful, very cultured lady, and no one had ever struck her in her entire life.

"Actually, I wondered at the time if anyone had ever struck Capucine. I don't believe they had. I've always believed that the greatest compliment I can pay a woman is to call her a lady, because, when I was brought up, I was taught that a lady is a woman for whom you have the greatest respect. Capucine is certainly that.

"She has something very special. She's made some very good films. And that face! I wish she'd done more work, because I really do enjoy watching her, seeing her do what she does on screen."

Barbara Stanwyck was to pass away only a few weeks before Capucine fell to her death.

Capucine originally came to Hollywood in 1960. She was quickly heralded as a star in the tradition of Garbo. After a few movies, however, she returned to Europe. In 1981, she returned to Hollywood to do a "Hart to Hart" television episode, and again, in 1985, to appear in "Murder, She Wrote." In 1989, she told a reporter from a Hollywood tradepaper, "I'm weary, always weary, these days. I'd like to work, but the enthusiasm is gone. But then, so are the opportunities," she added with a touch of irony.

Her father was John Barrymore, her mother the poet

Michael Strange. Diana Barrymore was educated in private European schools and given "too much, too soon," as she entitled her autobiography. She was given too little, however, of love, security and self-confidence. In her autobiography, she tells about her difficulties as an adolescent, her many love affairs, her three marriages and her descent into drunken isolation . . . and about her unsuccessful suicide attempts.

Toward the end of her life, she fell in love with a man she must have known she could never have, the playwright Tennessee Williams. It became an obsession. Williams, with his compassion for twisted human beings, was kind to her. He had befriended her after seeing her in a production of his play, *The Garden District* (which was filmed as *Suddenly, Last Summer*). But Williams attempting to help Barrymore stay off pills and booze was ludicrous. The playwright, at the time, was at his worst.

At age thirty-eight, the tempestuous sometimes stage and screen actress succeeded in escaping from a life she could not handle. On Monday, January 25, 1960, her maid found her dead in her $200 a month, two-and-a-half room brownstone apartment she rented on East 61st Street in New York City. Her bedroom was strewn with bottles of tranquilizers and sleeping pills, as well as empty liquor bottles. The New York coroner listed her death as a combination of alcohol and sleeping pills.

Remember Auntie Em in *The Wizard of Oz?* Clara Blandick became a recognizable face in the movies of the '30s and '40s. Eventually, the parts ceased, however, and Clara decided on a dignified exit in 1962. She dressed in her finest clothes, carefully made up her face, and arranged her hair in an elegant Gibson girl bun before she lay down on a couch in a hotel room in Hollywood, put a soft blanket over herself and slipped a plastic bag over her head.

Dorothy Dandridge, beautiful and talented, began performing professionally at the age of four, when she and her sister Vivian became known as "The Wonder Children." She made her movie debut in 1937 in the Marx Brothers classic *A Day at the Races*. In the '50s, she was virtually the first black movie star, with starring roles in *Carmen Jones* and *Porgy and Bess*. But the number of roles available to her were limited. By 1965, she was broke and deeply in debt, having lost her money in a get-rich-quick oil investment scheme. A week before Thanksgiving, she was found dead in her apartment on Fountain Avenue in West Hollywood from an overdose of barbituates. Her bank account contained two dollars.

Bella Darvi was born in Poland in 1928. She grew up in France and was incarcerated in a concentration camp during World War II. In 1951, Darryl F. Zanuck and his wife Virginia became interested in the young girl who was christened Weiger, gave her the name Darvi—a combination of Darryl and Virginia—and brought her to Hollywood. After three disappointing movies, the Zanucks deserted her and her contract with Fox was terminated.

Having acquired a taste for movie making and its rewards, she went back to Europe and tried to make it in French and Italian films. But nothing worked. She also ran out of money, but gambled incessantly.

Bella Darvi attempted suicide in 1962, in 1966, and again in 1968, but failed at that, too. However, in 1971, she succeeded. On September 17th, she was found in her Monte Carlo apartment, dead for over a week. The gas jets on the stove were wide open.

Irene Gibbons, known professionally only as Irene, designed costumes for numerous films and was Metro-Goldwyn-Mayer's costume designer during the 1940s. But times changed and demands with them. By 1962, when she was sixty years old, her husband was ill and she was broke. Irene jumped to her death from the top floor of the Knickerbocker Hotel in the heart of Hollywood. Sadly, she left a note apologizing to the other guests at the hotel.

She was called "The Body," when the former showgirl and band vocalist became a starlet in the early '40s. But

Marie McDonald's career never really took off in spite of appearances in about a dozen movies. Most of her publicity stemmed from scandals and seven weddings—a couple of them to the same man. In 1965, at the age of thirty-two, she stopped trying to make it, either as a star or a wife, and turned to the exit provided by an overdose of pills.

Brief fame followed by obscurity and self-inflicted death has become the Hollywood suicide staple. Maggie McNamara is an example, as well as being something of a mystery. Born in 1928, she was a teenaged fashion model, studied drama and dance, and made her Broadway debut in 1951 by replacing Barbara Bel Geddes in *The Moon is Blue*. In 1953, she repeated the stage role on the screen and was nominated for an Academy Award. She was a star. Fox signed her to a contract, but, after making *Three Coins in The Fountain* and *Prince of Players*, she simply disappeared, returning only once to play a supporting part in *The Cardinal* in 1963. She earned a living as a typist in an office and was forgotten until February of 1978, when she was found dead from an overdose of sleeping pills.

Gail Russell had an intriguing beauty in Hollywood films of the '40s. Dark-haired and blue-eyed, Gail was discovered as a high school student in Santa Monica and made an impression in *Wake of the Red Witch, The Uninvited, The Unseen* and *The Night Has a Thousand Eyes*. In spite of her success, however, Gail was never able to conquer her extreme stage fright which became an uncontrollable monster that drove her to alcohol. She was arrested many times for drunk-driving, each arrest bringing unwanted headlines. But her career received its death blow when a tabloid story linked her with John Wayne. Interestingly enough, the scandal did not cause even a dent in Wayne's popularity. After a few years of loneliness and no work, she was found dead in her apartment, empty liquor bottles standing guard. She was thirty-six years old.

It was not known whether it was suicide or an accident when the thirty-eight year old, green-eyed, female star of *Guns of Navarone, Don't Go Near the Water* and *Tunnel of*

Love died in 1972 from an overdose of drugs and alcohol. Gia Scala's career also suffered from her dependency on alcohol, which had led to several arrests. As in the case of Inger Stevens, her neighbor on Woodrow Wilson Drive, she also had attempted suicide a few years earlier.

On September 8, 1979, the body of actress Jean Seberg was found on la rue du General-Appert in the sixteenth arondissement of Paris in the back seat of her car, a white Renault. Beside her body was a bottle of barbituates, an empty bottle of mineral water and a note in French for her son:

"Diego, mon fils cheri, pardonne-moi. Je ne pouvais plus vivre. Comprends-moi. Je sais que tu le peux et tu sais que je t'aime. Sois fort.

Ta maman qui t'aime."

Seberg had been dead for ten days, during which time her second husband, Romain Gary, Diego's father, enlisted the help of close friends to search for her. Seberg at the time was married to her fourth husband, Ahmed Hasni. "We looked all over—certainly not expecting to find her dead," says Pavla Ustinov, a member of the search party.

"She was like a little girl in many ways. Chronically, drawn to the underdog, always picking up strays—cats, dogs, bums. She was one of the sweetest people I've ever met. Sweet and vulnerable and incredibly supportive of just about anything, often not for her own good," Pavla continues.

"What I don't understand is why the media treated her so harshly when others get away with far worse things than just being naive and not quite in touch with reality at all times. The media seem to have a flair for zeroing in on those individuals without malice who may be maladjusted—and finishing them off."

Perhaps it is not just the media, perhaps that is how many of us are? Perhaps that is what we unconsciously teach our children: how to be cruel and to whom it is safe to be cruel. Certainly the head of FBI had learned that lesson well.

"I blame J. Edgar Hoover for her death," Pavla says, "not to mention many other deaths and misfortunes." She is referring to the repeated questioning of Jean Seberg by the FBI regarding her ties with the Black Panther party, of which she—along with Jane Fonda, Marlon Brando and many other Hollywood celebrities—was an ardent supporter.

Diego, Seberg's son by the brilliant statesman/novelist Romain Gary, had been delivered by Caesarian. While resting after the birth, Jean translated documents from the Black Panthers into French and began her autobiography, calling it *Twinkly*, a nickname given by Black Panthers to stars who supported them.

When Jean became pregnant again, it was reported in *Newsweek*, as well as *The Hollywood Reporter*—and consequently picked up by papers around the world—that a member of the Black Panther Party was the father of a child "of a certain pregnant American film actress." The insinuation, which couldn't have been clearer, was made while Jean was having problems during her pregnancy.

Earl Anthony, whose explosive autobiographical book dealing with the Panthers and the FBI, *Spitting In The Wind*, had just been published, said, "Jean Seberg was a sweet girl with a big heart. She donated the use of her name and a bit of money to the Panthers, but she was never really involved as deeply as some of the others. And I would have known if she was ever involved with any of the Panthers personally, on a romantic level. She wasn't. I think the FBI's Cointelpro harassment of her was a simple matter. She was the ideal All American white girl from the Midwest, from a fine middle-class family, what they call the salt-of-the-earth family. Hoover, and a lot of the white agents, couldn't stand the idea of her supporting the Panthers. They spread a rumor that she was having affairs with us, that she was pregnant by a member of the Panthers. It was all in their heads, imagination run amok."

A lot of factors may have contributed to the mental state of Jean Seberg at the time of her death. Perhaps it began as far back as her first movie, *Saint Joan*, about which Richard Widmark has said that it was the worst experience of his career, largely due to the brutal manner in which the director treated Jean. The Iowa-born girl had been plucked from anonymity at age seventeen and chosen from 80,000 applicants from the world over for the title role, a storm of publicity making her famous before the shooting began. Then the film turned out to be a flop, critically and commercially. She fared a bit better in *Bonjour Tristesse*, but her acting career did not really come alive until she went to France. In Jean-Luc Godard's directorial debut, *Breathless*, she was impressive as an American beatnik in Paris. Another contributing factor may have been that she seems to have carried her identification with her roles to an extreme, not the least the role in *Lilith* opposite Warren Beatty. She may have, at times, fused with her parts to the point of losing sight of her own personal identity.

The harassment by the FBI, the ugly clouds surrounding the parenthood of her child and the subsequent death of little Nina three days after her birth left Seberg defenseless. Distraught by the ugly rumors, she flew back to Iowa with the body of the dead infant, having the open casket on public display in her hometown of Marshalltown for two days before the funeral, obviously to prove the skin color of the little one.

Jean Seberg kept on living, and even married a couple of more times. But friends tell how every year, around the August birthday of her dead child, whom she had fought like a tigress to try to save and who even before birth had become a racist issue, Jean tried to commit suicide. Everything had turned to a lie, a fake. "Nothing protected her . . . not even her own skin, " a friend remembered.

Hollywood's men were not exempt from the incredible triumphs followed by frustration and misfortune. The picture is all too familiar.

Clyde Buckman shot himself to death in 1955 in the men's room of a Hollywood restaurant. He had eaten a hearty dinner there and did not have money enough to pay the check. Who was he? He began as a screenwriter at Warner Brothers, worked as a gagman for Buster Keaton and, later, as Keaton's screenwriter. He then directed comedies featuring Harold Lloyd, Laurel and Hardy and W.C. Fields. In 1935, his career ended. Professional failures, combined with marital problems, continued to plague him. He ended it all with a shot from a pistol borrowed from Buster Keaton.

Two dramatic suicides were those of Lou Tellegen and Max Linder. Both men committed hara-kiri.

Tellegen was born in Holland in 1881, was Sarah Bernhardt's leading man in Paris, and settled in Hollywood in 1913, one of the screen's most handsome leading men. He published a book, *Women Have Been Kind*, in 1931 and became a film director before the pain of being forgotten and unwanted killed him. In 1934, he died after stabbing himself in the chest, stomach and throat with a pair of gold scissors. Around him were his scrapbooks, posters and photographs from his days of glory and fame.

Max Linder, an actor and director, was born in France in 1883. By 1910, he was best known as an international comedian. In 1914, he was a soldier during World War II and was a victim of gas poisoning, never regaining his physical or mental health after the war. He moved to the United States in 1916 and made a number of films, including *The Three Must Get There*, a parody of *The Three Musketeers*, but returned to Europe in 1923. The bodies of Linder and his wife were discovered, side by side, in a Paris hotel in 1925. A note indicated they had entered into a suicide pact.

James Murray's trouble-filled, thirty-five years ended in 1935, when, completely drunk, he jumped—or fell—into the Hudson River. He had gone to Hollywood intent on an acting career. He was handsome and convinced of his own talent. But the parts he managed to get were tame, until King Vidor cast him as the lead in *The Crowd*. Leading roles followed, but he was soon unable to perform due to chronic alcoholism. For years after his death, King Vidor worked on a screenplay about the short, tragic life of this promising young actor.

George Reeves's first movie role was Brent Tarleton in *Gone with the Wind*. During the '40s, he played supporting roles and minor leads. Then the '50s brought the role of Superman in the popular television show. Reeves gained enormous fame—and even managed to act in a few movies in addition to his duties in the series.

When the last "Superman" episode was filmed in 1958, Reeves discovered that he was typecast as this fictional character. He found it difficult to find work. He told an interviewer, "It's like Hopalong Cassidy trying to get a job in white ties and tails. The producers just won't give me a job. They take one look and say it's impossible."

As his proceeds from "Superman" dwindled, Reeves was forced to make a living by exhibition wrestling. Humiliated and despondent, he committed suicide by shooting himself on the night he was scheduled to fight his first match.

Grant Withers' name is not exactly a household word, but he did make headlines in 1930 when he eloped to Yuma, Arizona, with a pretty, seventeen-year-old named Loretta Young. Withers was the tall, handsome star of about two hundred Hollywood films during the late 1920s. After the marriage was annulled just months later, Withers played smaller and smaller parts until he fell into obscurity. In 1959, he took an overdose of sleeping pills.

One of the most bizarre suicides has to be that of Albert Dekker. Dekker was an established Broadway actor by the time he made his screen debut in 1937 in *The Great Garrick*. The tall, husky thespian became a popular movie villain with the title role in *Dr. Cyclops*, but everything seemed to turn sour with the years. He felt that neither his professional nor his private life flourished.

On May 7, 1968, the actor was found dead and a macabre scene greeted the police. He was found hanging in his bathroom, bound and handcuffed. There was no suicide note, but he was reportedly dressed in a woman's flimsy silk robe and had words—supposedly taken from unfavorable reviews of his acting—written in bright red lipstick all over his body.

Charles Boyer represented the gallant Frenchman. The elegant, sexy man with the rich voice thrilled movie audiences all over the world. He was a matinee idol in France and reached Hollywood in 1934, where he established a solid career starring opposite such female stars as Ingrid Bergman and Greta Garbo.

But, in 1978, the eighty-year-old actor felt it was time for a final curtain. He took his own life with an overdose of barbituates two days after his wife of forty-four years died. Incidentally, their only child, Michael, committed suicide in 1965.

In 1937 two witty Englishmen, David Niven and George Sanders, worked together in a picture. Niven later quoted Sanders as saying, "I will have had enough of this earth by the time I am sixty-five. After that, I shall be having my bottom wiped by nurses and suffer being pushed around in a wheelchair. I won't be able to enjoy a woman anymore, so I shall commit suicide."

He did exactly that in 1972—at the age of sixty-five.

The elegant, and very British, George Sanders came to Hollywood in 1936. He was a cultured man with a strong sense of cynicism which was often utilized in his screen roles and equally so in his private life.

Sanders was a bit of a loner and could get into deep black moods. But women were fascinated by him and he married four times, including Zsa Zsa Gabor, Benita Hume and, briefly in 1970, his former sister-in-law, Magda Gabor.

In 1972, he arrived in Barcelona. It was a cold, rainy day. He rented a small room in a modest hotel overlooking the sea. He downed five bottles of Nembutal with a bottle of vodka, leaving this written note:

"I am committing suicide because I am bored. I feel that I have lived long enough. I leave you all in your sweet little cesspool and I wish you luck."

A movie career just didn't work out for Ross Alexander. He was groomed for stardom by Warner Brothers in the early 1930s with disappointing results. Rapidly, his career dwindled to roles in B-pictures. In early 1935, he married a stage actress named Aleta, who had moved to Hollywood in search of fame. Four months after their wedding, Aleta went into the yard surrounding their home and shot herself. She was despondent because Hollywood wasn't interested in her as an actress and her husband Ross, fighting increasing disappointments in his once promising career, was already spending nights with other women.

Ross married actress Anne Nagel nine months later, but, exactly four months after that marriage—and less than two years after his first wife's suicide—Ross Alexander killed himself with the same rifle Aleta had used. He was thirty years old and had just completed a role in the picture *Ready, Willing and Able*.

Actors are not the only people in show business who end up with their own personal demons, unable to function with any other means in which to make a living. It has happened since the movies were in their infancy.

George William Hill began his career at the age of thirteen as a stage hand for D.W. Griffith, then worked as cameraman and screenwriter before turning to directing in the early 1920s. He directed several scripts written by the prolific female screenwriter Frances Marion and they wed. The marriage was short-lived. They separated, reconciled, separated again and divorced in 1931. More and more, Hill depended on alcohol to get through the day. His crew covered for the popular and undeniably talented director, but his studio did not trust him and threatened to fire him for good.

In 1934, Metro-Goldwyn-Mayer head, Irving Thalberg, although worried about Hill's alcoholism, admired his remarkably realistic style and superb visual sense enough to give a chance to direct Pearl Buck's *The Good Earth*. The screenplay was by Frances Marion. Hill went to China with a crew, filmed some exteriors and seemed to be in control of his drinking problem. When he returned to Hollywood, Thalberg summoned him to a production and story conference. The director arrived dead drunk.

Frances Marion was there and instructed her chauffeur to take Hill to their oceanside home in South Venice, where he was living alone. At some time during the night, Hill shot himself in the head with his army revolver.

Who can understand the tragedy that lived in the tiny body of actor Michael Dunn. He was born a dwarf in 1934 in Oklahoma, but nurtured strong ambitions to be taken seriously as an actor rather than as some kind of circus freak. In the early 1960s, he impressed audiences in *The Ballad of the Sad Cafe*. His film debut in *The Ship of Fools* in 1965 earned him an Oscar nomination. His acting career ended abruptly in a hotel room in London in 1973 during the filming of *The Abdication*. "A possible suicide," read the official reports.

Everybody knew Nick Adams as a nice guy. He took great pride in his celebrity friendships. "Movies were my life," he said, remembering his dream of becoming a big movie star. "You had to have an escape when you were living in a basement. I saw all the Bogart, Cagney and Garfield pictures—the ones where a guy finally gets a break against all the odds in the world. That was my meat."

Nick hitchhiked to Hollywood from Pennsylvania, but every door remained closed. He enlisted in the Coast Guard in 1952. Two years later, he returned and managed to talk himself into a part as a sailor in *Mister Roberts*. He became friends with James Dean and appeared in *Rebel Without a Cause*. His biggest break came when he was cast as Andy Griffith's buddy in *No Time for Sergeants*. Even after he had been in more than a dozen movies, Nick always had a willing ear for the troubles of the famous and was always ready to do a favor, run an errand or whatever—he remained a fan.

He became nervous and jumpy. A close friend said that Nick felt he was being snubbed by some celebrities. His doctor prescribed a calming sedative. On February 7, 1968, thirty-six year old Nick Adams was found dead from a medical overdose in his home in West Los Angeles.

One hour and twenty-five minutes into the new year of 1972, Peter Duel, thirty-one, ended it all with a single gunshot into his right temple. The bullet passed through a window and landed on the floor of a carport across the street from Duel's Hollywood Hills home.

The popular co-star of "Alias Smith and Jones" had spent New Year's Eve at home with a girlfriend, Diane Ray, watching television. They watched first his show and then a baseball game. She was in the bedroom when he entered, took a pistol from a drawer, said, "I'll see you later," and left the room.

Shortly afterward, she heard a shot. He was lying next to the Christmas tree in the living room of the rustic, two-bedroom home, with a snub-nose .38 caliber revolver at his feet.

In an interview four weeks earlier, he had said that acting in a television series "is a big fat drag to an actor who had any interest in his work. It's the ultimate trap. It isn't the work that tires you, it's that it's all such a dreadful bore that it makes you weary."

About a week before his suicide, police learned, Duel had lost an election to the Screen Actors Guild board of directors.

Hollywood has always been rough on its child actors. The Oscar for "outstanding juvenile actor of 1949" went to twelve-year-old Bobby Driscoll. The popular child star played the boy who witnessed a murder in the thriller *The Window*. In 1950, he played Jim Hawkins in *Treasure Is-*

land; in 1951, he starred in *When I Grow Up* and, in 1952, in *The Happy Time*.

The two latter titles turned ironic as Bobby became a teenager. He only worked occasionally. Unable to adjust to his changing life situation, he began taking drugs, became a heroin addict and was arrested several times.

In 1968 the happy times were over. The thirty-one year old former child star died in an abandoned tenement in Greenwich Village of a heart attack, induced by taking Methadrine. His identity was unknown for a full year.

Another example of a child actor who could not get adult roles and was unable to accept a life outside of show business was Scotty Beckett. He began his career at age three as a regular member of *Our Gang*. In films, he played young Jolson in *The Jolson Story* and many other child and adolescent roles. He made his last movie in 1955 and then could not get even a small part; he couldn't make it as an adult actor. Scotty lived an embittered life and committed suicide when he was thirty-eight years old.

Or take Bobby Harron, one of several children of a poor Irish family. He was a messenger boy at Biograph when D.W. Griffith promoted him to actor in screen parts requiring a gentle, slightly wistful masculinity. He had a boyish charm, people liked him, he was sincere—and he played in movies with the Gish sisters and Mae Marsh.

But then someone new came on the screen. In this case, it was handsome and virile Richard Barthelmess. Roles that had previously gone to Harron were now given to Barthelmess. Lillian Gish gushed that Barthelmess had "the most beautiful face of any man who ever went before the camera." For Bobby Harron, these words cut deep.

On the eve of the East Coast premiere of *Way Down East*, in which Barthelmess scored one of his greatest triumphs, Bobby Harron was found in his New York hotel room, dead from a self-inflicted gun shot. Griffith immediately told reporters that the pistol had discharged accidentally and that there was no reason on earth for young

Bobby to commit suicide. The press lamented the young actor's accidental death, but Bobby's friends knew he was despondent because Griffith had found another protégé.

Some stars could handle dark disappointments and do something else with their lives. For others, the road came to an abrupt end with no conceivable alternatives, except to end it all through suicide.

CHAPTER 6

The Way Some People Die

Her husband sentenced her to death.

"I hope the bastard burns in hell," she said.

Amanda Blake was the beloved "Miss Kitty" of "Gunsmoke," American television's long running success. Her words were for Mark Spaeth, her fifth and last husband, whom she had married in 1984. Spaeth was a real estate developer from Texas and had been bisexual most of his life, something he neglected to tell Amanda. Two months before the marriage, he had been diagnosed as having AIDS. The disease soon became fullblown, the marriage ended in divorce and Amanda moved from Austin, Texas, where they had been living, back to Los Angeles.

Spaeth died in 1985 and, two years later, Amanda was diagnosed positive. She tried to keep it a secret and moved to a wildlife ranch outside Sacramento, California. In 1988, she had a bout with pneumonia, lost weight, was in constant pain and began to experience severe depression. In July of the next year, bitter and suffering, she entered the hospital in Sacramento under her real name, Beverly Neill, and died on August 16, 1989

His death remains a mystery.

He was born Rudolpho Alonzo Raffaele Piere Filibert Guglielmi di Valentina d'Antonguolla, but the world will always remember him as Rudolph Valentino. Handsome and mysterious, he became a star dancing the tango. But the actor with an air of menace and mysteriousness about him on the screen was rather passive privately, allowing women—and his studios—to run his life and make major decisions for him.

Valentino's second marriage to tall, mysterious Natacha Rambova created headlines when it was discovered that he had not yet received the final divorce decree from his first wife, Jean Acker. Valentino landed in jail for bigamy, but, when he stood trial, he pleaded, "I would do it again to make her my wife." It took the jury two minutes to acquit him.

As his movie success continued with *The Sheik* and *Blood and Sand*, women continued to faint in the aisles, even though Natacha was creating a barrier between he and his audience. Valentino placed all of his affairs in his wife's hands and even heads of studios had to arrange for appointments through her—sometimes weeks in advance. When she tried to change his screen image with *Monsieur Beaucaire*, the studios rebelled and Paramount got an injunction against him, preventing him from appearing in films.

Still in charge, Natacha arranged for a two year dancing tour. Finally, the two went to Europe, where they found European film producers just as afraid to hire him because of the injunction. They returned to America and Valentino, forced by money problems, caved in to the producers. Natacha, rebuffed by producers at handling Valentino's affairs, went to Europe in a huff and divorced him.

In August of 1926, the thirty-one year old clutched his stomach and collapsed in his suite at the Ambassador Hotel in New York. He was taken to the Polyclinic Hospital, where he went into a coma and died on August 23rd. The official report was that he had a perforated ulcer and a ruptured appendix. Media rumors soon contrived a story that someone had placed a "Micky Finn," namely sodium amytol, in his drink.

His funeral caused a near riot, as more than 20,000

people fought to get a last glimpse of the dead screen idol. Women of all ages shrieked, screamed, moaned and tore their clothing in public. The Italian Fascists sent a guard of honor; the Anti-Fascists were there to fight them off. One twenty-year old fan in London took poison and died surrounded by photos of Valentino. "With his death, the last bit of courage has flown," she wrote in her suicide note. Later, another woman, the mother of two children and also surrounded by photos and articles, tried to commit suicide by drinking iodine and shooting herself. She was saved at the last minute.

Natacha came back from Europe to declare that she had received "spirit messages" from the actor, who, according to her, had met Caruso "on the other side." Jean Acker made a statement to the press that she did not believe a word of it. Natacha retaliated by publishing her memoirs—including conversations with Valentino from "Beyond."

Long after his death, women continued to claim to have given birth to Valentino's babies. Since his death, as recently as 1990, self-proclaimed psychics have made claims of being in contact with Valentino.

Valentino left a debt of $200,000. He had earned more than five million dollars during his brief career. The anniversary of his death brings an annual visitation of fans to his Hollywood Memorial Park grave site.

John Garfield, the cynical, defiant young man who consistently scored in movies where he played the "young man from the other side of the tracks," died in 1952 at the age of thirty-nine. Newspapers carried the story that he had died in the middle of having sex in an unfamiliar bed. Friends felt that he was unable to deal with his blacklisting as a result of the House UnAmerican Activities Committee. After establishing himself in *He Ran All the Way, Force of Evil, Gentlemen's Agreement, The Postman Always Rings Twice, Destination Tokyo* and many other films, Garfield was the son of poor Jewish immigrants. He grew up on New York's lower East Side, his life filled with problems, brawls and delinquency. When he won a debate contest sponsored by *The New York Times*, he received a scholarship to drama school and, in 1938, was signed by Warner Brothers to star in the movie *Four Daughters*.

During the committee investigation, he refused to name friends as communists and was forced to leave Hollywood. He had returned to the New York stage when he died.

The dead beauty in the bathtub was exotic star Maria Montez. At thirty-one, she had had a heart attack while taking a bath, but the rumor mill continued long afterward to hint at suicide.

The daughter of a Spanish consul to the Dominican Republic, she was a model who began her career playing bit parts at Universal in 1941. Although her talent was not obvious, her beauty was. She soon became popular in a series of "tits and sand" movies of the 1940s and behaved accordingly. Her offstage life began to sharply mirror on on-screen performances in films like *South of Tahiti, Arabian Nights, White Savage, Follow the Boys, Cobra Woman, Gypsy Wildcat* and *Siren of Atlantis*.

The Thief of Venice in 1950 was her last major film. Within months, she was found dead, just as her career was beginning to decline. Following her death, however, she became something of a cult figure.

In only four short years in Hollywood, Laird Cregar made over a dozen movies, culminating with *Hangover Square* in 1945. His roles in *Holy Matrimony, Heaven Can Wait, Blood and Sand*, and *Charley's Aunt* portended a bright career for the polished young actor. At six-foot-three, he was the smallest of six brothers and his broad proportions made him perfect for roles ranging from Jack the Ripper to the Devil himself. Cregar did not start in films until 1940; he was twenty-four years old.

Four years later he was dead, having eaten and dieted

himself to his death. He had a tendency to gain weight easily and he became enormous. Then he dieted, losing a great deal of weight, only to begin eating again. These seesaw eating binges and crash diets weakened his heart and caused his untimely death at the age of twenty-eight.

Mayo Methot, a sexy blonde actress was a heavy drinker. In 1938, when she became Humphrey Bogart's third wife, alcohol flowed freely at their wedding reception. Actor Micha Auer appeared from behind a huge wedding cake and danced stark naked for the guests. Throughout their marriage, Bogie and Mayo could often be seen in Hollywood's restaurants or at lavish parties, invariably drunk.

Like many actors who play tough men in the movies, Bogart would often encounter his share of the "let's see how tough you really are" types. Instinctively, he avoided physical fights, preferring the verbal insult instead. Mayo, according to the Hollywood grapevine, was the opposite. Many stories of her physically attacking one of Bogart's hecklers are legend. Bogart nicknamed her "Sluggy."

Mayo was equally at ease taking on Bogie at home, and the Hollywood press soon christened them "The Battling Bogarts." Many of these attacks came about because of her jealousy of his leading ladies. Once Mayo slashed her wrists and another time she set fire to their house.

Following a particularly rough night, during which the two had used each other as targets with old whiskey bottles, Bogart ran from the house and headed for a nightclub. The doorman pointed out that his back was bloody. In the heat of battle, Mayo had stabbed Bogart in the back with a kitchen knife and he had not even noticed.

As Bogart continued to become more successful, his married life began to concern both agents and studios. Mayo's jealousy of Ingrid Bergman and other co-stars increased as the years of drinking began to take their effect. By the time of *Casablanca*, Mayo had almost completely lost her looks. By this time, Mayo had not acted in years and was a bloated drunk. But Bogart remained loyal and defended her at every turn. "She is an actress who is not working. She has talent, but does not get to use it. That's a tough situation," he kept repeating to friends.

Then, in 1944, came *To Have and Have Not*—Lauren Bacall. And this time there was good reason for Mayo's jealousy. Bogart had fallen absolutely and irrevocably in love with his new, young leading lady.

Bogart knew he was in love with Bacall, whose years masked a maturity far beyond her age. The outcome of their relationship was never in doubt. The only question was how to tell "Madam," as he now called Mayo. Bogart understood the frustration of his wife's stalled career, particularly since she had been a very capable actress. He also knew she was capable of real violence, not only to others, but to herself. His conflicting emotions, many of them centering on Bacall's youth and what he could offer her, allowed Mayo to realize that this time something was truly threatening their marriage.

Suddenly, Mayo promised to stop drinking.

Bogart, incredibly loyal, decided that in all fairness, he had to give her another chance. The couple spent the summer at Newport; Mayo really tried to behave; and Bogart stayed away from his young love.

The Bogart/Bacall pairing became big box office and in October 1944, the two began shooting *The Big Sleep*, their second movie. Bogart was determined to give Mayo a chance and to remain honest and scrupulously fair.

But the thought of Bogart working with Bacall was too much for Mayo; she began drinking again. After another of their classic fights, Bogart stormed out of the house—directly to Bacall.

Mayo implored through the press that she loved Bogart and would do anything to get him back. She knew that her marriage was floundering and tried desperately to hang onto it. It was a desperate situation, characterized by her drinking, hangovers and self-destruction. When Mayo was finally brought to the hospital, Bogart returned. He remained until a final Christmas celebration turned into a punching, flailing and shouting melee.

Bogart left, this time for good.

Mayo's dreams, of both her career and love, were hopelessly shattered. She left Hollywood and went to Oregon, where she was born. She drank and drifted. Six years later, Mayo Methot was found dead, alone, in a motel room.

David Niven characterized Mayo: "A classic, Hollywood casualty."

The suicide of Romy Schneider, Germany's "Shirley Temple," shocked the world. With both of her parents famous German actors, Romy got her start at an early age, eventually making over sixty films. She made her Hollywood debut in *Good Neighbor Sam* with Jack Lemmon, but, in the 1960s, the parts dried up and she moved back to Europe.

In July 1981, her fourteen-year-old son David was accidentally killed. Romy had divorced his father, the West German director/actor Harry Meyer-Haubenstock (who committed suicide in 1979) and since remarried. On May 30, 1982, at the age of forty-three, she died by her own hand in her Paris Apartment. She was separated from her second husband and had a daughter Sarah, who was four at the time of her mother's death.

How do you spell heroine? Too often, in Hollywood, the answer has been heroin.

Alma Rubens was a beautiful star of Hollywood silent films, but the public did not know that the star of *The Price She Paid* and the first production of the Edna Ferber classic *Showboat* spent most of her time and money in the drug market.

After the raven-haired beauty was confined to the California State Hospital for the Insane for a period, she was returned to her home, only to be arrested again for possession of morphine. But doctors found her too ill to be confined and she was allowed to remain at home until her death in agonizing pain at the age of thirty-three.

Another such heroine was Jeanne Eagels, a delicate blonde beauty with an equally delicate spirit. An actress from the age of seven, she is remembered for bringing her gossamer qualities to the role of Sadie Thompson in *Rain*. She made several other films, but died in 1929, barely thirty-five years old.

CHAPTER 7

Murder Most Foul

A murder mystery is a reliable staple in the entertainment industry. Under the blazing California sun, where emotions are heightened and extremes are the norm, real life murder mysteries are, if not common, at least frequent. One of Hollywood's most notorious murder mysteries still remains unsolved.

In 1922, William Desmond Taylor, a suave, attractive, bachelor—and a man who loved the ladies—had become a prominent director in the rapidly growing film industry. President of the Screen Directors Guild, he had already helmed several Mary Pickford vehicles. But Taylor had directed his last picture.

On February 2, 1922, William Desmond Taylor was discovered dead in his home. He had been shot in the back, either as he was seated at his writing desk or as he returned from escorting Mabel Normand to her car. Normand, a beautiful actress with a reputation for wildness, was seen leaving Taylor's home minutes before the murder. An overturned chair was the only evidence of a struggle.

But Normand was not the only one who was rumored to be in the house the night of his death. Mary Miles Minter, beautiful—and very young, may also have visited him during the last hours of his life.

Other evidence at the scene had been obliterated by the time the police were called to the scene. As usual, when a celebrity was involved in anything out of the ordinary, the studio was informed before the police. By the time the police arrived, nearly a dozen friends, relatives and studio representatives were on the scene and the house had been stripped of anything incriminating.

Police found Taylor lying on his back on the floor, a bit too perfectly arranged. The first doctor on the scene believed he had died of a gastric hemorrhage until the body was rolled over and a bullet hole was discovered in his back.

In the weeks after the murder, rumors abounded, compounded by the actions of the participants, their relatives and their studios. Mary Miles Minter's mother, Charlotte Shelby, sent telegrams to the news media, declaring that her daughter was innocent and looked upon Taylor only as a father figure. Since Minter's film image was one of purity and innocence, she faced ruin as the investigation revealed several of her pictures in the house and a dainty silk handkerchief with her three initials in a corner.

Mabel Normand's career also received a hefty blow from the press.

A determined police investigation found itself mired down in persistent rumors that lead nowhere: stories of Taylor's surviving brother of which they could find no trace, vague hints of a strange love cult and secret rites, gossip involving the firing of a former employee and a fruitless search for him through several states, and a suggestion of two foreign cigarette stubs found outside the house. But, as one lead after another failed to materialize a killer, jealousy—of one kind or another—loomed stronger and stronger as the primary motive for the killing.

William Desmond Taylor was born William Cunningham Deane Tanner in Dublin on April 26, 1877. Although most of Hollywood was unfamiliar with his background, the investigation of his murder revealed that he had abandoned a wife and child in New York early in his life, and the daughter, now nineteen, had recently contacted him. But, from his arrival in California, Hollywood hostesses loved him and women fell easily in love with him. He was also a man of stature in his profession. He directed over forty films, including *Huckleberry Finn, Anne of Green Gables, Sacred and Profane Love,* and *Morals.* Jesse Lasky called him a "gentlemanly British director, considered a model of decorum and propriety."

Mabel Normand. twenty-eight at the time, was a radiant and talented star in the Mack Sennett Company. She and Sennett had been on the verge of marrying several times, but the wedding plans were always postponed. Although they were obviously in love, Mabel had once discovered Sennett in bed with one of her friends, Mae Busch, and felt she could never trust him.

Mabel and Australian-born Mae Busch had worked together as advertising models in New York. When Mae was stranded when a promised musical did not materialize in Los Angeles, Mabel took her into her apartment and got her a job with Sennett. Sennett and Mabel had set the wedding date for June. Shortly before, Mabel went to Mae's new apartment, obviously suspicious, and found Sennett and Mae in a nude embrace.

From that time, Mabel became Madcap Mabel. Concerning Sennett, she remorsed, "I have forgiven him. It's just that he's somebody else." Between wild parties, she attempted suicide several times, admitting "I don't belong in this world."

Sennett, a sardonic, exuberant and sometimes cruel man, would continue to make films with Normand, but comics working as her co-stars knew they had to be careful. Flirting with Mabel was a quick way to get fired by Sennett, who still loved the small, dark, piquant girl he called "as beautiful as a spring morning."

Spunky Mabel would probably have been able to recover from the lurid stories in connection with Taylor's death, even with reporters' hints about her all-night partying and drug use. But she suffered another scandal almost immediately. Hollywood millionaire Cortland S. Dines was found shot to death, with Mabel's chauffeur holding a pistol belonging to Mabel. The two suspicious deaths delivered deadly blows to Mabel Normand's career. She made her last picture in 1923 and, after that, appeared only in Hal Roach comedy two-reelers.

Mary Miles Minter was nineteen according to studio records, although Charlotte Shelby had been consistently lying about her daughter's age for years, subtracting a year here and there. On stage at the age of six, she had been driven by her mother until, finally, she became a film actress at age ten. She obviously loved and admired William Desmond Taylor and he returned the affection—although he still sent flowers to Mabel Normand three times a week. Although Charlotte Shelby tried to alter appearances after the murder, Hollywood had little doubt that Mary and Desmond had been lovers.

The morning after the murder, Minter suffered a severe case of hysterics and rushed to the gates of Taylor's house, much to the horror of her studio executives. She was finally persuaded to go into seclusion. Mary Miles Minter made her last movie, *The Trail of the Lonesome Pine*, the next year and disappeared into virtual withdrawal for the rest of her life. In her later years, she became a virtual cripple. In 1981, she was found beaten, bound and gagged in the driveway outside her cottage. Her house had been stripped of all its contents and mementoes. Three years later, at age eighty-two, she died. Even her death could not still the Taylor rumors, as unconfirmed reports indicated that there was a daughter living in Switzerland, born at a time that would make it possible for William Desmond Taylor to be the father.

At Taylor's funeral, Mabel Normand collapsed at the casket. Later, she told police that she had gone to Taylor's house at the Alvarado Terrace Apartments, 404 B South Alvarado Street, the night of his murder. Her chauffeur had driven her, so that she could pick up a book Taylor had found for her at Robinson's Department Store. She said she stayed approximately half an hour, estimating her arrival time at around five minutes past seven. "We chatted, mainly about books," Mabel told the police.

Taylor was shot in the back a little before 7:45 p.m.

The press had a field day with the intricate details of Taylor's murder, both factual and fictional. There was conjectures and speculations about narcotics, orgies, and missing love letters from Minter, Normand and several other actresses. Some were found several days later in one of Taylor's boots.

Both Mabel Normand and Mary Miles Minter were officially cleared of suspicion. However, their careers faded into oblivion because of the association with murder.

William Desmond Taylor's killer has never been found. Neither has the murder weapon. Hollywood rumor, however, has presented many killers from innocent betrayed to protecting mother to jealous lover.

In several reports, District Attorney Woolwine, who investigated the case, indicated that he knew very well who had fired that fatal shot. "A person I could never convict," he is reported to have told people close to him.

The murder of lovely Karyn Kupcinet is another of Hollywood's unsolved mysteries.

On the evening of November 30, 1963, around seven o'clock, actor Mark Goddard and his wife Marcia decided to check on their friend, twenty-two year old actress Karyn Kupcinet. Karyn had not answered her phone since she had attended their house for dinner the preceding Wednesday. Karyn's apartment was located at 1227 1/2 North Sweetzer Avenue in Los Angeles. Directly off Sunset Strip, it was located on a court with eighteen other apartments, most of them rented by young actors and actresses appearing in movies and television.

Outside Karyn's door, Mark and Marcia found three-day-old newspapers, two magazines and a copy of Henry Miller's *Tropic of Capricorn*. A small Christmas wreath adorned the door.

There was no light coming from the apartment, but Mark and Marcia could see through a crack in the window that the television was on. Thinking Karyn might have fallen asleep, they tried the door. It was unlocked.

Karyn was lying on her side on the living room couch. Flecks of blood covered her face and a pillow. She was naked. The only clothing in the room was a bathrobe thrown over the back of a chair. She was wearing no makeup.

A brandy snifter which had been used as a cigarette container, a coffee cop and a lamp had been knocked to the floor. Nearby lay a spoon, a pink and white panda and a small throw pillow. A partially empty cup of coffee was on a side table.

A bright girl from a warm, stimulating family in Chicago, Karyn had come to Hollywood two years earlier determined to make it as an actress. Her father was nationally known columnist, Irv Kupcinet. Popular among her friends, she read existentialist books and was fascinated by anthropology. Her career had begun to take shape; she had appeared with Jerry Lewis and had just finished a role in the "Perry Mason" television series.

The police investigation uncovered that Karyn had been murdered, manually strangled with such force that a small bone in her neck was broken. She had been dead about three days.

Karyn and actor Andrew Prine had been seeing each other for some time, although they were in the process of breaking up when she was murdered. Prine, along with three others, took a lie detector test given by the police department in order to prove their innocence.

In addition, Prine described another side of Karyn's personality. She had once concealed herself in the attic of his home when she found he was dating another girl. Also, both he and Karyn received threatening letters, pasted together. Police examined the letters he still had in his possession and determined that Karyn herself had sent them, probably in a desperate attempt to bring the two of them closer together.

The mystery of young Karyn's death was never solved.

Her death deeply affected those closest to her.

No discussion of Hollywood murders would be complete without some discussion of the grim "Black Dahlia Case," a name coined by several of the reporters who covered the case. The name itself may possibly be the very reason the case created headlines and without which the incident of a naked, severed and mutilated girl from Maine might have been forgotten. As it was, the "Black Dahlia" became the center of the public's attention.

Elizabeth Ann Short was a twenty-two year old, would-be actress, and sometimes prostitute, who always wore black. She was found butchered on a vacant lot on Norton Avenue near 39th Street in central Los Angeles on January 15, 1947.

Just after her body was found, more than 2,000 policemen and spectators rushed to the scene. Gradually, information surfaced. She had been one of the thousands of girls who migrated to Hollywood in the 1940s, hoping to become a star. Instead, unable to find work in the business, she lived in a house with other out-of-work girls and gradually turned to prostitution.

The grim condition of the body brought out the worst in the psychotic element. More than fifty psychopaths confessed to the murder and more than four hundred suspects were questioned. All were found innocent. At one point, the actual murderer supposedly called the *Herald Express*, confessing to the crime and mailing Short's Social Security card and other identification to the paper to prove it. He never reappeared and the person who took the call could not definitely identify the voice as either male or female. From the condition of the body, the police were positive that the killer was mentally deranged, but the assailant's sex could not be determined. The coroner's examination suggested cannibalism as well.

The grisly act set off a rash of useless suggestions: a person from Alabama suggested that Short's corpse be buried with an egg in her hand and the killer would be found within a week; another requested her right eyeball so that it might reveal the final image of the murderer when photographed. Several women took advantage of the murder and accused men with whom they wanted to get even of the murder.

One young, curly-haired combat veteran was reported by another soldier. He had returned from a forty-two day furlough with bloodstains on his clothes and his pockets stuffed with newspaper clipping about the murder. "I could have done it," he confessed. "I tend to get rough with women when I'm drunk." Checking the facts, the police cleared him and sent him to a psychiatrist.

Throughout the case, it was comparatively simple for the police to find if a confession was false; there were so many specific details about the murder that only the murderer could have known. A few days following the murder, two members of the Los Angeles homicide squad returned from lunch to find they had been reported by a waiter who had overheard them discussing the case over their meal.

The case of the "Black Dahlia" was never solved.

The Hollywood murder of screen lover Ramon Novarro was a cold, senseless act committed over a few dollars.

Three men epitomized perfection in the hearts of the female moviegoer of the silent film era: Rudolph Valentino, John Gilbert and Ramon Novarro.

On October 31, 1968, the sixty-nine year old Novarro was cruelly bludgeoned to death in his Hollywood Hills home by two young brothers: Robert, twenty-two years old, and Thomas Scott Ferguson, only seventeen.

Novarro's male secretary found him lying naked on his king-sized bed the following morning. Furniture was broken and overturned in both the living room and the bedroom, indicating that the slightly-built actor had struggled against the two younger men who had entered his home on Halloween evening.

Novarro was born Ramon Samaniegos in Durango,

Mexico on February 6, 1899. The eldest of thirteen children, his father was a dentist who early moved his family to Mexico City, where Ramon attended college, studying music, French and English. He also became an avid movie fan and, along with his brother, soon took off for Los Angeles. They arrived on Thanksgiving Day of 1916 with ten dollars between them. Four years of lean years followed, during which Ramon worked as an extra in movies.

When the rest of the family joined them in Los Angeles a few years later, Ramon and his sister, Carmen, began to dance professionally. Their tango skills drew attention from film makers, and they were given bit parts in *The Four Horsemen of the Apocalypse*.

Soon, the roles increased in size: in *The Prisoner of Zenda*, Ramon Samaniegos had fourth billing. Ramon Samaniegos became Ramon Novarro and continued with *Trifling Women* and *Where the Pavement Ends*. The public liked him immediately. "Novarro acts by thought rather than gesture," said one critic.

Novarro never stopped studying music and singing, at one time contemplating a career in opera. When the movies turned to sound, he made *Devil May Care* in 1929 and re-enforced his position as one of Metro-Goldwyn-Mayer's top stars.

In the mid 1930s, he left film to concentrate on stage work, returning in 1959 to play character roles, mainly villains. He continued to work in television roles, guest starring on "Bonanza" and other shows.

Novarro guarded his private life carefully throughout his career. He never married. At one point in his life, he had withdrawn to a monastery, giving birth to rumors that he would eventually seek a monastic life. He experienced bouts with pleurisy and was known to drink heavily.

In an occasional interview, he was known to disapprove of the way romance was portrayed in modern movies. "Today's movie heroes are not gentlemen," he once said. "We were more romantic. Subtler and, therefore, sexier. There is too much vulgarity, and even violence, in love scenes now."

The question of Novarro's homosexuality became a focal point of his murder investigation. His two young killers were hustlers from Chicago.

"He was framed," stated Anita Page, who appeared with Ramon in *While the City Sleeps*. "Ramon was a gentleman." Another female star declared that she knew of many women who were sexually involved with him. Obviously, Novarro's appeal, like that of Valentino, attracted both sexes.

At his funeral four days after his death, more than one thousand people passed by Ramon Novarro's open coffin. The two hustlers, Robert and Thomas Scott Ferguson, were sentenced to life terms in prison on October 27, 1969.

Carl "Alfalfa" Switzer was shot for fifty dollars. A member of the beloved "Our Gang," he was a freckled youngster with a squeaky voice, who became an actor at an early age and joined the series in 1935 when he was nine. He stayed with it until 1942.

As he grew older, he appeared in minor roles in *A Letter to Three Wives, State of the Union* and *Pat and Mike*, but the parts continued to shrink.

For a while, he worked as a hunting and fishing guide in northern California, finally becoming a bartender. In January, 1959, at the age of thirty-four, he was shot in a drunken brawl in his home, originating over a dispute concerning a fifty dollar debt.

Although Victor Kilian's name might not be familiar, his face would immediately be identifiable to millions. Television viewers will recall him as the "Fernwood Flasher" in "Mary Hartman, Mary Hartman."

Kilian actually starred in vaudeville, stock companies, and Broadway before making his screen debut in *Gentlemen of the Press* in 1929. From then until the early 1950s, he made well over sixty films, including *Gentlemen's Agreement, Spellbound, The Ox-Bow Incident, Reap the*

Wild Wind and *Tovarich*. Kilian specialized in playing the character role of an angry villain.

In 1979, just as the eighty-eight year old actor was enjoying a new career in television, he was killed by intruders in his Hollywood apartment.

Frank Christi was another character actor, playing villains in *The Godfather* and appearing on television in "The Rockford Files" and "Charlie's Angels." As the roles became few and far between, the actor turned to other means to make a living.

Christi was gunned down in the carport of his Hollywood Hills home.

Police suspected that the killing was the result of a drug deal which had turned sour between dealers and the out-of-work actor.

On the evening of February 13, 1976, Sal Mineo parked in the carport of the apartment building on Holloway Drive in West Hollywood where he lived. He was returning home from rehearsals of a play, *P.S. Your Cat Is Dead*, in which he was to play a bisexual burglar.

As he walked toward his apartment, he was attacked and stabbed through the heart with a knife. When he cried out, the man scurried away and a neighbor came running. Attempted mouth-to-mouth resuscitation proved of no avail and the young actor was dead at the age of thirty-seven.

Sal Mineo was born in the Bronx section of New York on January 10, 1939. Beginning on Broadway, he graduated to playing the young prince in *The King and I* before moving to Hollywood and a string of troubled youth roles. He was twice nominated for an Academy Award, in 1955 for *Rebel Without a Cause* and in 1960 for *Exodus*.

In 1969, he would return to New York to direct *Fortune and Men's Eyes*.

With Mineo's death, the Hollywood rumor mill had a feast. Insinuations, guesses, and speculations filled the press and television. A local Los Angeles television newscast based its reports almost entirely on unsupported gossip. Most of the rumors that centered on Hollywood's favorite subject, his sexuality, were pure fabrication. One friend stated flatly, "Sal was not kinky. He was not into leather and/or S&M . . . He was a sweet and very loving man. And he took himself and his profession very seriously."

Mineo's family and friends were aghast at the seamy stories that circulated. At the funeral services held in New York five days after the murder, Chips Meyers eulogized his brother-in-law, "He lived his life with courage, abandon, humor, style and grace. His art—what he created—will always stand. Nothing can take it away from him."

Detectives from the West Hollywood's Sheriff's Office had a strong lead on Mineo's murder from the beginning of the investigation, but were extremely careful about disclosing the nature of the investigation. There had been a series of ten strongarm robberies in Sal's neighborhood within a month's period—all involving one man, using either a knife or gun—and the police had identified a suspect and questioned his relatives.

Police were searching for Lionel R. Williams, a twenty-one year old former pizza delivery man. Williams' girlfriend told the police that he had come to her apartment the night of Mineo's murder with apparent bloodstains on his jacket, ranting a wild story about having stabbed someone. Later that same night, when she and Williams were watching television, a photograph of Mineo was flashed on the screen and Williams blurted out, "That's the dude I killed."

Police still did not have enough evidence to arrest Williams for Mineo's murder, but they waited.

Early in 1977, Williams was arrested in Inglewood, California for outstanding traffic tickets, but was extradited to Michigan authorities to face charges of forgery. Williams went willingly, but Los Angeles detectives advised

Michigan authorities that he was a suspect in the Mineo case. While serving time for forgery in Calhoun County jail in Michigan, Williams talked to a cell mate about committing the Mineo killing. Three days before he was to be released, he learned the Los Angeles County Sheriff's Office had filed charges and was seeking to extradite him to California. They had connected him to a small, yellow Dodge Dart seen leaving the scene of the crime.

Williams was extradited to Los Angeles and charged with the murder of Sal Mineo on May 4, 1978. Despite his boastful prison talk, he pleaded not guilty. It took the jury a week to reach a verdict, but, in March of 1979, Williams was sentenced to a minimum of fifty years, receiving consecutive sentences of five years to life for the second-degree murder of Mineo, nine counts of first-degree robbery and one count of second-degree robbery.

In the early afternoon of June 29, 1978, actress Virginia Berry went to the Scottsdale, Arizona, apartment of actor Bob Crane. The apartment was provided by the Windmill Dinner Theater, which was presenting Crane and Berry in a production of the play *Beginner's Luck*. Berry and Crane planned to go over a videotape of a previous performance of the play in order to smooth out some staging problems. Thinking the actor might still be asleep, she tried the door and found it unlocked.

A few minutes later, the apartment complex resounded to her hysterical screams.

Bob Crane, former star of television's "Hogan's Heroes," had been murdered. His body was sprawled across the bed. He had been struck on the head several times; his features were hardly recognizable. An electric cord was wound around his neck.

Police were summoned and two officers, Lieutenant Ron Dean and Detective Dennis Borkenhagen arrived on the scene within minutes. Questioning an almost hysterical Virginia Berry, they ascertained that Crane drank very little and was not known to do any drugs. When he did drink, he preferred vodka and orange juice. They found two bottles, one of scotch and one of vodka, on a coffee table in the living room.

As neither Crane's wallet or watch was missing, robbery was immediately ruled out as a motive. Crane's 1977 Chevrolet Monte Carlo, supplied by the theater, was still parked in front of the apartment complex.

The contents of Crane's closet, however, drew the interest of the police and was the trigger for a series of rumors and media speculations—building the death into national front page tabloid news. There was a great deal of expensive camera gear, including chemicals and containers for a portable darkroom. The set-up would have allowed the actor to develop his own pictures in a bathroom.

Several large, glossy photographs were found, along with several albums of mounted photographs. All the pictures were sexually explicit, many of them of nude women and others—taken with a delayed timer—of Crane involved in various sex acts with different women. Video equipment in the apartment indicated that Crane not only photographed his sex acts with numerous women, but also videotaped them.

At the time of his death, Bob Crane was forty-nine years old. It was an ironic ending for a man who had always called himself "one of the lucky guys."

Originally, he had intended to be a drummer. "Like Gene Krupa, who was my hero," he declared. "I had this fantasy. I'd be at the Paramount Theater in New York and Louis Prima's drummer falls sick. The theater manager asks, 'Is there a drummer in the house?' I run up on the stage and—bang—instant fame! Lucky me—it never happened. However, I practiced the skins for a few years and then drifted into other things."

What he drifted into was radio. After having worked with the Connecticut Symphony and traveled with several east coast dance bands, he became a radio announcer at several stations, starting in 1950 at WLEA Radio in Hornell, New York. He earned thirty-seven dollars a week.

Crane arrived in Los Angeles in 1956 and replaced Ralph Story on a radio morning show. From there, he moved into acting and became a regular on "The Donna Reed Show." He made several movies, including *Mantrap*, *Suspended* and *Return to Peyton Place*, but he achieved permanent popularity in the television series "Hogan's Heroes."

At the time of his death, Crane was married to actress Patricia Olson, who had played Hilda in "Hogan's Heroes."

The autopsy revealed that Crane had been struck twice on the head, possibly as he was sleeping. The second blow killed him. The electrical cord had been placed around his neck after he was dead. Because of the force necessary to deliver the deadly blow, the coroner's report suggested the killer was male.

Checking Crane's movements, police found that, following his performance the night before, he had gone to a nightclub with an old friend from Los Angeles and two women. He had left them at a coffee shop about two-thirty in the morning, saying that he was going home. The friend went directly to the airport to catch his flight home, but phoned Crane before his plane left. Crane was at his apartment, apparently alone and in a good mood.

Gradually, the investigation came to a halt. When it was learned that a third book of mounted photographs—showing the actor engaged in intercourse with three different women—was missing from the apartment, it was theorized that a husband or one of the women may have been the murderer, but the Bob Crane murder is still unsolved.

Thelma Todd was a curvaceous blonde with a figure that set male imaginations churning. Born on July 29, 1905, she led her early life much in the style of a Doris Day movie: she was a schoolteacher, who did part time modeling.

In the mid-1920s, she entered a beauty contest—and won. Thelma decided that she might like Hollywood and soon found that Hollywood indeed liked her. In 1926, *Fascinating Youth* was her first film and she continued to work steadily, building her career with a number of comedy shorts. Soon nicknamed "The Ice Cream Blonde," she was a clever blend of beauty and brains, quickly becoming famous for her witty delivery of wisecracking lines. Later, she had her own comedy series and shone in a couple of Marx Brothers and Laurel and Hardy comedies.

Unfortunately, the wisecracking Thelma was not as worldly-wise as her screen roles indicated. As she turned thirty, she opened a nightclub on the Pacific Coast Highway across from the beach. Thelma owned the property, but her partners really ran the business. The nightclub was successful and Thelma seemed satisfied.

Gambling had been illegally introduced into several clubs around Hollywood at the time and had proved to be financially profitably. Thelma's partners—rumored to be little more than mobsters—were anxious to reap new profits at the club. But Thelma, with her ex-schoolteacher background, had developed a puritanical streak and would have nothing to do with the idea.

Thelma Todd died of carbon monoxide poisoning in her parked Packard convertible. Her elegant evening gown and mink coat were supposedly splashed with blood and torn. Further details of her death are clouded in mystery.

Shock and tragedy cling to two Hollywood deaths. Although Bill Buckland had his family roots buried in old Hollywood and Marvin Gaye was a modern phenomena, both were killed by their own fathers.

The Bucklands were one of the first families of Hollywood. Vida Buckland was a gorgeous actress who appeared in movies in the early 1930s. Wilfred Buckland was one of the finest art directors in films. Their son, Bill, had been a playmate of Doug Fairbanks, Jr., Jesse Lasky, Jr., the DeMille girls and other offspring of Hollywood aristocracy.

Bill attended Exeter Academy and Princeton and was

the toast of debutante parties, but, as he grew older, began to develop mental problems. His mind became more and more fragmented and he was finally given shock treatment.

When Vida Buckland died of cancer, Wilfred Buckland took care of his son alone, but, as the years passed, he found himself less and less in demand as an art director. He was also reaching an advanced age. As he reached his eightieth birthday, Wilfred Buckland obviously decided that he could not stand having his son spend the rest of his life in a mental institution once he himself had died. Penniless, and all but forgotten, Wilfred shot his son in the head while he slept, and then fired a second bullet into his own.

The gentle, talented singer, Marvin Gaye, holds a prominent place in the history of American pop music. He helped put Motown on the map, chalking up thirty-four hit singles and fifteen more duets with female singers Mary Wells, Kim Weston, Tammi Terrell and Diana Ross.

Marvin had started singing at the age of three in his father's church. He also played the organ and started as a session drummer. Berry Gordy, Jr.—whose sister he would later marry—signed Marvin to a Motown contract in 1961 and his first hit came with "Stubborn Kind of Fellow" in 1962.

In 1971, the album "What's Going On?" showed a maturing social awareness, and, after "Let's Get It On" a few years later, Marvin became inactive. Torn most of his life between "the flesh and the spirit," he retreated with his psychological problems.

In 1982, Gaye made a comeback with the hit single "Sexual Healing," and began to share his emotions and psychological wounds with his listeners. Although he remained distant outside of his work and did not behave like a pop star, he knew how to communicate through his work and, at the same time, cleanse himself. He won two Grammy Awards.

One day before his forty-fifth birthday, on April 1,

1984, an argument arose between Marvin Gaye, Jr. and his father in their home in the Los Angeles Crenshaw district. The argument escalated into violence and seventy-year-old Marvin Gaye, Sr., a minister, shot his son twice in the chest.

Marvin Gaye's father was found guilty of murder and given five years' probation.

Diana Ross dedicated her hit, "Missing You," to Marvin Gaye, Jr.

"Albert Salmi gave in to the demons that caused his nightmares." That is the only way his friends can explain the series of events that led him to murder his wife and then take his own life.

Salmi was a loner, with an intensity that had served him well in his career. Of Finnish descent, he was born in Coney Island, New York. Equally at home on the stage and in films, he appeared in several Broadway productions, including *The Rainmaker* and *Bus Stop*, and at least twenty feature films.

Specializing in rough character types, he was equally at ease in television and appeared in more than a hundred and fifty shows, including "Gunsmoke," "Petrocelli," and "Lawman."

For twenty-five years, he had been married to Roberta who had big eyes, a cute freckled face and soft femininity. Roberta was a true romantic and there could have been times when she felt that reliable, steady and at times darkly moody Albert was not the dashingly romantic hero of which she dreamt. For years, she planned to write a love story with herself as the slightly disguised heroine, that would, in her words, "top every romance I have ever read."

According to their friends "Albert was nuts about her." Most believed that the two enjoyed a nearly perfect marriage, except when he drank too much.

The family had moved from Hollywood to Spokane, Washington. Salmi was increasingly given to lengthier and lengthier bouts of depression because offers for acting roles were becoming few and far between. Roberta then filed for divorce.

On April 23, 1990, Albert Salmi, sixty-two, shot Roberta, fifty-five, in the kitchen of their home. Her death was instant. A neighbor saw Roberta's body through the window and called the police, who discovered Salmi's body in an upstairs den. He had shot himself.

The demons had claimed a basically good man.

Hollywood families may, indeed, be a danger to themselves, but they can never compare with the dangers stars face from the world outside their profession and from the very people who idolize them so completely.

The phenomenon of fan hysteria spans the range from intense adoration to intense hatred, a dark side easily dominated by dangerous obsessions. When a star stands as a symbol, he or she also becomes a focus of public opinion. Often, a disagreement with that focus will be enough to turn an adoring fan into a maniacal killer.

As the world gasped, John Lennon was gunned down on December 8, 1980 outside the Dakota apartments where he lived in New York City. Mark David Chapman, a pudgy, twenty-five year old, had flown from Hawaii specifically to fire the .38 Special handgun that cut short the life of a man who had earned world fame as a member of the Beatles. At forty, Lennon had just cut "Double Fantasy," his first album in five years. Psychologists stressed that Chapman was suicidal and may have believed he was Lennon and, therefore, was actually killing himself.

John Hinckley became fixated on actress Jodi Foster and attempted the assassination of President Reagan to impress her; Arthur Jackson stalked actress Theresa Saldana through fourteen states before he finally found her in Los Angeles and stabbed her eleven times; Michael Perry, an escapee from a mental institution who wrote to Olivia Newton-John and tried to get close to her, finally murdered five members of his own family.

Twenty-one year old Rebecca Schaeffer, who co-starred in the television series "My Sister Sam," had just been featured in the film *Scenes of a Class Struggle in Beverly Hills*. She was killed by a nineteen-year-old fan, who waited outside her apartment, finally ringing her bell and shooting her as she answered the door.

A twenty-six year old woman was arrested after sending more than 5,000 threatening letters to actor Michael J. Fox, insisting that unless he divorce his new wife, actress Tracy Pollan, both of them would die; a former mental patient shot and killed two unarmed Universal Studio guards who refused to admit him to see actor Michael Landon.

The threat and danger to stars has always been part of the Hollywood landscape. Barbara Stanwyck got court restraining orders, hired guards, and, finally, sold a house she loved and moved to a secluded neighborhood because an ardent fan followed her for years.

More recently, a former legal secretary was sentenced to two-and-one-half years in prison for violating a court order to stay away from performer Michael Jackson's house and stop representing herself as his wife; and television talk show host David Letterman has had his house broken into four times and his car stolen by a woman calling herself "Mrs. Letterman." A fifty-two year old farmer has been convicted of harassing singer Anne Murray; during a six-month period in 1989, he called her office two hundred and sixty three times.

Sharon Gless, formerly of the television series "Cagney and Lacey" and star of "The Trials of Rosie O'Neill," had her house broken into by an obsessed fan who held police at bay for five hours, threatening suicide. The break-in took place at 3:15 a.m., but luckily no one was in the house that Gless used as an office during the day.

Experts say that fans turn violent, not out of hatred, but because their romantic fantasies are unable to be fulfilled. A false bond is created, fostered by an "I see her every week. How can she not know me?" attitude. Celebrities who seem sweet and approachable are especially vulnerable to this psychosis because their unavailability becomes more frustrating, more intense.

The girl-next-door, the character created and championed by Saldana and Schaeffer, is in much greater danger than the portrayer of the eternal bitch.

RUDOLPH VALENTINO
The death of the screen's most popular Latin Lover allegedly was caused by a perforated ulcer and a ruptured appendix.

MARIA MONTEZ
The exotic "tits and sand" screen siren died of a heart attack while taking a hot bath.

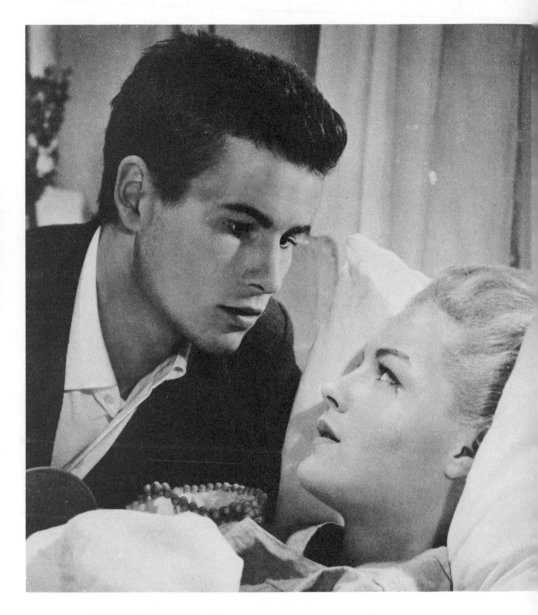

ROMY SCHNEIDER

Germany's "Shirley Temple" was so despondent after the death of her teenaged son that she killed herself in Paris at age forty-three. (Shown with Horst Buchholz in *Love From Paris*.)

WILLIAM DESMOND TAYLOR

His sensational murder case decades later still brings conjecture as to who really committed the crime.

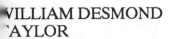

MABEL NORMAND

Madcap Mabel's career came to an abrupt halt when she became a suspect in William Desmond Taylor's murder.

RAMON NAVARRO
Two young Chicago hustlers brutally beat to death one of Hollywood's most adored stars.

SAL MINEO
Gay hatred was rumored to be the motive behind the fatal stabbing of Mineo; a young robber's confession belied these speculations.

BOB CRANE

It was discovered that the star of "Hogan's Heroes" starred in his own x-rated videos when police investigated his murder in a Phoenix, Arizona apartment.

MARVIN GAYE

An uncharacteristic argument led to his fatal shooting by the singer's seventy-five year old minister father.

FLORENCE BALLARD
  Self-destructive, she was the tragic Supreme, living on welfare after quitting the popular Motown group. (Shown here with Diana Ross and Mary Wilson.)

JOHNNIE RAY

A sweet, gentle and kind man, he "cried" his way to become the first true pre-teen idol. Shortly before his death in 1990, he said, "I've lived too long to be famous anymore."

BILLIE HOLIDAY

Drug addiction cause much of the tragedy th: filled the life of "Lady Day However, her style with song is legendary.

JANIS JOPLIN
She created herself with bizarre stories to the press, but an overdose brought a tragic end to a skyrocketing career.

JUDY GARLAND

Her marriage to Mickey Deans in London was barely covered by the press; Judy was "old news" and would be dead in just a few months. (Shown here with Deans and Johnnie Ray.)

AVA GARDNER

Whether it was Andy Hardy, the bobby-soxers' favorite crooner, or a bull fighter, Ava's marriages and affairs were fodder for the press mill. She tired of the attention and died alone in London.

MARILYN MONROE

Adele Jergens, playing Marilyn's burlesque mother, and the "Ladies of the Chorus" implore "Every Baby Needs a Da-Da- Daddy."

MARILYN MONROE
 John F. Kennedy's birthday bash at Madison Square Garden found Marilyn with her own special present for the President.

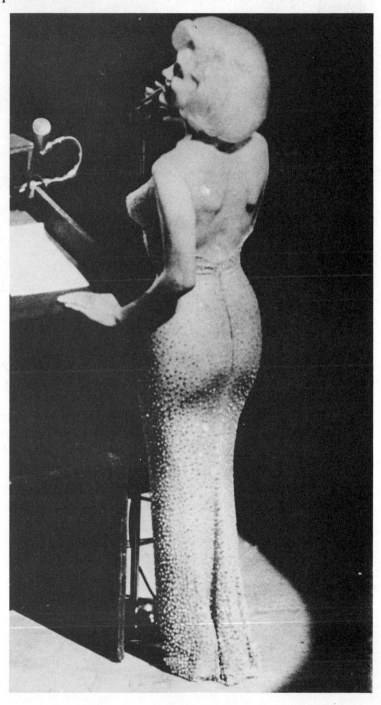

INGER STEVENS

The strain of keeping her interracial marriage a secret took its toll, and, officially, "The Farmer's Daughter" committed suicide when she was only thirty-five years old.

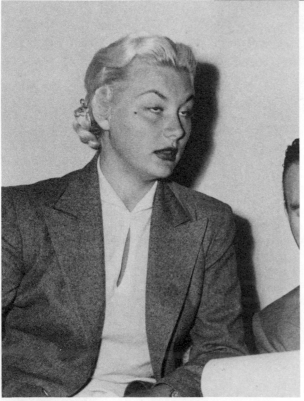

BARBARA PAYTON

After reading Payton's autobiography "I'm Not Ashamed," Barbara Stanwyck quipped, "She jolly well should be."

ROBERT WALKER
    He never stopped loving ex-wife Jennifer Jones and was unable to find peace and a fulfilling relationship with any other woman. (Shown here with Judy Garland in *The Clock*.)

ERROL FLYNN
He lived life on the edge and crowded ten lifetimes into one fantastic drinking spree.

DENNIS HOPPER
After hitting the depths of alcohol and drug abuse, Hollywood's original angry young man found his way back to an even more brilliant career.

CHAPTER 8

Caged Birds Sing

If the Hollywood studio system chewed up artists and spat them out—and it did—the record companies were worse. The old Hollywood moguls often went to extremes in protecting their stars, and seldom kicked them when they were down and out. But the record companies, the nightclub owners and the public seemingly delighted in building up recording stars, only to discard them with a vengeance at the first sign of a slip. A few recording artists lasted, but most enjoyed a few moments in the spotlight and were soon forgotten.

Hollywood is home to many singers who had one hit record years ago or even a single record that made it to the number one spot on the bestseller charts. Year after year, these artists keep looking for a new recording contract and try to keep their names alive by playing small clubs throughout the country, trying to recapture those few moments of glory again.

After World War II, the music industry moved from New York to Hollywood. It's center was on Vine Street, where the new Capital Records Building, a circular, high rise—with a stylus on top that made it appear like a very tall stack of giant records—was erected. The advances made in electronics after the war resulted in record players becoming affordable to most households, and most teenagers, and the new 45 rpm plastic records were suddenly very inexpensive.

There had always been popular singing stars with national and international followings. Since World War I, with rare exceptions, band singers were secondary to the bandleader in "star" status. That was all to change. The singers were to become more important than the "name" band they fronted.

Singers such as Frank Sinatra, Billie Holiday, Johnnie Ray and rhythm and blues queen Ruth Brown were fighters and, with the exception of Holiday, were among the survivors. In their era, as Johnnie Ray put it, "It was a form of slavery. You were bound by an iron-clad contract; somebody owned you and you never really knew who that someone was. You did what you were told and you didn't ask questions. We were caged birds who sang when we were told to."

Another factor that made singing stars different, and more vulnerable, from movie stars was that studio systems were set up to keep a protective wall between the movie star and the public. It worked—as long as the studio wanted it to work, that is. Before *People* magazine made it semi-respectable to report the private lives of movie stars, magazines such as *Life*, *Saturday Evening Post* and *Colliers* depended on the cooperation of the studio publicity departments for what often were cover stories.

The magazines cooperated, in turn, by overlooking misbehavior by favored stars from major studios. However, if a star went too far, a word to gossip mavens Hedda Hopper or Louella Parsons brought a mild public reprimand. And, if a star continued to act up, the studio would let the press know that they could play hardball. Sometimes, if it was a slow month, the magazine fabricated stories and it was easier to attack a singing star than a major motion picture star.

The "one hit record" phenomenon were not the only ones to have problems later on. Mary Wilson, formerly of the Supremes, could not get the interest of any major record company. Ruth Brown, known in the 1950s as "The Queen of R&B" and once called "the woman who built Atlantic Records," couldn't get a recording contract until she returned to Broadway in a hit musical revue. Johnnie Ray, the singer who is credited with bridging pop and rock 'n roll, was talking to a record company only a few weeks before his death with the intent of recording for the first time in a decade.

There have always been black singing stars—mostly blues singers such as Bessie Smith and Billie Holiday—who would draw a crowd—and sell records—without a "name" band playing behind them. But Johnnie Ray was the first white singer to become more important than the band. It didn't matter who played behind Johnnie because the fans came to see him.

The revamped record business after World War II was perfect for this new kind of singing star, who went into a sound studio and cut records; that was their business, what they did. In the days before rock 'n roll, a singer often recorded several cuts in an afternoon session and there was very little fussing around with the master; the band played the song all the way through, the singer sang it all the way through without stopping, and that was that and it was recorded.

Records were important, but it was in the clubs and concert halls that a singer was measured. No matter how big a recording star a singer was, in those days an endless series of one night stands was the rule. The road work was rough, devastating on some performers—a different club, a different hotel room, a different city, night after night for weeks, sometimes months. It's still not much better and for some, country singers especially, no better at all. However, today stars such as Madonna and Cher have almost total control of their careers, their bookings, and surround themselves with professionals—people who know their business.

Having it and then not having it, it's an old story.

Florence Ballard was the tragic Supreme. She came from a Detroit housing project called Black Bottom. There were twelve children in the Ballard family. Florence was born on June 30, 1944. Her father worked for Chevrolet, but died when she was very young. She had a couple of girlfriends named Diane and Mary. Like the other children in the neighborhood, they spent a lot of time on the streets and saw drugs, gangs, prostitution and fights.

"Luckily, neither one of us fell in love with a boy who was a pimp or a gang member," she said once. "The girls who did ended up in trouble. But we never got around to that because we were too wrapped up in other things by the time we started looking at boys."

The girls loved to watch television. They saw how some people were dressed, how they lived, what they owned. They could not fail to notice that the people living in televised luxury were white. Hardly a black could be seen on television in those days except for Eddie "Rochester" Anderson on "The Jack Benny Show."

The girls fantasized about futures that were gloriously different from their present reality. All they did was accompanied by music. On Sundays, it was the church organ. The three sang in the choir along with their families. During the week, they sang wherever they happened to be—along with the radio, with other kids. Music was as important to them as the air they breathed. And, somehow, in the back of their heads, there was hope in the harsh reality of their lives.

They learned all the new songs they heard on the radio. "Rock 'n roll was much more important to us than boys." Groups formed here and there, groups that sang together. One group of boys who called themselves the Primes began to get local bookings. They told a promoter of some girls in the Brewster Housing project that sound pretty good. And the Primettes were formed.

The first Primettes included Mary Wilson and Florence Ballard—but not Diane Ross. Florence was, by then, less close to Diane than to Mary. She was a quiet girl who dreamed of becoming a nurse. But she was the one who had first thought of starting a singing group and she had asked Mary and two other girls, Barbara Martin and Betty

Anderson, to join in. Betty lasted a very short time and that's when Mary talked the others into letting her friend Diane have a chance to join the group. Florence and Barbara were concerned about making the right choice, now that the door to performing had opened just a little. They decided to give Diane—or Diana as she began calling herself more and more—a last test and the four of them went to a backyard and sang. People gathered around. These people felt music in their souls and were harsh critics; they knew what was real and what was not. Little by little, fingers began to snap and feet began to tap. The girls had their first triumph—and earned three dollars.

Life was not easy for Florence. Since her father died, her oldest brother was head of the family. He believed strongly that a solid education was the only way out of the ghetto. When Florence's grades slipped, he blamed music for taking too much of her time. He ordered her to quit the group and concentrate on studying. Since he was closer to her age than a parent, he was tougher to fool.

Diana began pleading with him. It took several weeks before he gave in. Had it not been for the other girls' insistence that they would not move on without Florence, who had instigated the whole thing, chances are that Florence would have submitted to her brother's wishes. Even then she was less determined than Diana and Mary. It happened that she missed a rehearsal now and then.

The Primettes sang at dances, block parties, church and civic functions. They all knew that the small successes that nourished their dreams did not mean that they could escape the real world. Florence planned to become a nurse as her "real job."

However, on a spring day in 1960, four high school girls in identical dresses—Diana, Mary, Florence, and Barbara—walked into Berry Gordy's Hitsville USA recording studio in Detroit. Berry Gordy thought they had a nice way with a song but told them to finish high school, get their diplomas and come back. This was not good enough for Diana. She managed to get a job as an office girl at the studio during the summer and talked Gordy into using the Primettes as background singers now and then. Three of the four girls were ecstatic. The fourth, Florence, went through a period of confusion and uncertainty.

Florence did not have much encouragement from her family. Her belief in the future of the group wavered and she felt she should concentrate on studying to become a nurse. She also pondered the words of a music teacher of hers, who kept telling her that if she wanted to sing, she ought to sing classical music. Her gifted soprano voice lent itself well to arias. Florence was also more interested in school than the others and later, she said, with some regret, "I think I could have been an opera singer. If I only had more training . . . As it was, none of us learned to read music."

Barbara Martin fell in love and got married right after high school. Diana, Mary and Florence decided to go it alone and Florence came up with a new name for the three of them: The Supremes.

Still, she didn't show up for occasional singing dates at local hops.

Berry Gordy kept gaining in strength and influence and he now changed his company's name to Motown (from Detroit's nickname, Motor Town). With a certain amount of hesitation, he gave The Supremes a contract and put Smokey Robinson to work with them. Berry Gordy literally took over the lives of his artists and the three girls had to attend daily courses in his Artists Development Department. They kept singing, taking turns singing the lead. Finally, Gordy felt that Diana's voice was the most commercial of the three. Mary felt that Florence should have been the one to sing lead. "Flo had a powerful gospel voice," she said later. In "Let Me Go The Right Way," however, Florence does sing the lead.

They worked, became a bit recognized but success was slow in coming. Florence talked to Mary about going to Chicago and joining the Navy as a Wave. She went through periods of depression, during which she became even quieter than usual.

Then it happened. Success hit and hit big. Flo said at the time, "Even when I listen to our records, they give me a feeling of wanting to move, of wanting to get up and dance."

The lives of the three girls changed radically. Life was exciting. Barely twenty in 1964, the girls made three hundred thousand dollars. In 1965 they made more than twenty-five television appearances. All three bought houses for their families, on the same street, in one of the nicer black sections of Detroit.

Strangely enough, their lives acquired a kind of sameness: a puzzle of limousine rides, airplane trips, night clubs, press and radio interviews, hotel rooms, dressing rooms, and always someone prodding them to "hurry up, time to move on." They were on constant display. They had to be eternally charming and a little mysterious. Even Europe became a blur of stage doors and dressing rooms and spotlights. There was exhaustion and a special kind of loneliness.

There were occasions when they felt hampered by their lack of education and inbred sophistication—when they simply felt uncertain, awkward, and a little lost. Florence tended to withdraw at such times.

By the middle of 1966 it became clear that Florence Ballard had some real problems. Unable to express what she felt, she was constantly exhausted and began to seek refuge in a drink or two . . . or three. It was as if she never really adapted to the life The Supremes had to lead.

Several years later, Diana Ross said, "It got to be too much for her. She wouldn't show up for recording sessions, she wouldn't show up for gigs . . . Yes, she was drinking . . . But the problems were mainly in her head. She was tired. She didn't love what she was doing. She wanted out. Florence was buying a lot of furs and fancy cars, but she wasn't having fun."

Diana and Mary were exasperated with her but they also loved her, and they tried to understand. Berry Gordy kept warning her that unless she changed, he would have to do something drastic. She would shape up for a short while then, but her behavior was becoming more and more self- destructive.

Gordy thought of replacing her, but Diana and Mary protested. They kept hoping that she would pull herself together and get better.

In the beginning of 1967, Berry Gordy knew he had to replace Florence Ballard. In order not to upset anyone, he said that it was "temporary—until she gets her head together."

Florence's pride was hurt and she wrote to Diana and Mary that she was quitting. For good. She left the group in the summer of 1967.

Not long after that, she married Thomas Chapman and made her home in Detroit, where her twin daughters were born on October 13, 1968. A little later she had another daughter. She commented at the time of her departure from the group that certain things were more important than money, that she was sick and tired of traveling and wanted to settle down and raise a family.

But, on February 22, 1976, a message of sorrow came from Detroit: Florence Ballard was dead at the age of thirty-two of apparent cardiac arrest.

She and her husband were divorced, and she was alone with three children to support. It was said that she lived in a rundown apartment, spent most of her time watching television with her mother and children, and was on welfare.

Two years after she had left The Supremes, she had spoken of making a come-back as a solo artist. She did sign with ABC Records and released a couple of singles ("Love Ain't Love," "It Doesn't Matter How I Say It [It's What I Say]"), but they fared poorly.

In 1971, she filed a law suit for eight million dollars, charging that Motown and The Supremes had not paid out any royalties since she left the group four years earlier. Motown countered that a large cash settlement had been made when she quit, and that she at that time had relinquished all future claims. Florence lost the suit.

In the beginning of 1975, the first hint of scandal touching The Supremes was played up by the newspapers. "Former Supreme Living On Welfare" was the headline splashed over the front pages.

"I've been through so much . . . so much anguish over so many thing," she told reporters. "Now I just let things happen. I hope things will turn out all right, but I just don't know."

The publicity seemed to help a little. A few offers came in but when it came down to taking advantage of them, she lost her courage.

Rumors circulated that she had worked for a while as a maid, but that she had gone back on welfare. Both Diana and Mary tried to help her, but Florence refused. She was a strange mixture of unhappiness and pride.

Both women were genuinely shocked and saddened by the tragic fate of their childhood friend. But Diana said, "Did I cry? Oh yes, I cried. People tried to help Florence. I tried to help her. Sometimes I wanted to get hold of her and shake her, but nothing seemed to work . . . She had it all and she threw it away. She quit The Supremes, we didn't quit her . . . Florence was very important in my life, but I'm not dead. She did this to herself." Diana told a friend that she went through a period of guilt, then she became angry. Finally she was deeply sad.

Mary said, "I'll be damned if I'm going to end up like Flo . . ."

Sadly enough, only about a month before she died, Florence had called Diana to tell her that she was finally realizing that she had mainly herself to blame for everything that had happened to her. She spoke optimistically about "getting things together in my head."

Mary arranged the funeral—Diana was there, Berry Gordy was not. Very quietly, Diana set up a trust fund for the three small children.

Johnnie Ray, Jim Morrison and Elvis Presley are excellent examples of singers who got too close to their audiences, and got burned—or burned out—as a result. Writer and anthropologist Ray Locke, who has been close friends with several singing stars, believes that intimate touch is the key, both to a singer's success and downfall, "In one concert tour, Madonna will be nearer to—and in touch with—more people—fans—than a movie star, say Warren Beatty, might interact with his entire life. And live concert tours, for all the precautions that are taken—and sometimes that amounts to very little actually—offer the opportunity for more things to go wrong. One wrong move and Madonna may also, in one night, cause more animosity among her fans and, by extension, the press, than Warren might in his entire life. It really is a rather scary thing when you think about it."

Locke continues, "For instance, I met Jim Morrison about a year or so before The Doors came into existence. He often crashed with my next door neighbors, a couple of flight attendants . . . Most of the time, Jim sort of slept and hid from the landlady in someone's apartment. It was some months later that he met Ray Manzarek, who was putting together a group of musicians who would eventually become The Doors. Jim was very hesitant about becoming a part of a rock group. He was more into his writing. Of course, he had no idea that he was going to become this pop idol. Later, we talked about that one afternoon at a bar on Santa Monica Boulevard in West Hollywood. The audience reaction fascinated and scared the hell out of him at the same time. And, Jim being Jim, he was intrigued by the idea of seeing how far he could take an audience. He was getting off on it and it was leading to a situation that neither of us quite comprehended at the time.

"I really don't know what it is, this sort of love-hate thing fans get for singers, the ones that become pop idols. I still don't understand it, but it always seems to be there, some sort of primal emotion. Morrison's audiences saw him as some funk god. It didn't matter that he wasn't a very good singer. He was a poet and a damned good one.

He could sell his poetry, as lyrics, and himself. The audience bought the package. For some reason, they wanted to destroy it—the package, the image, and hence the performer—at the same time.

"I don't know why, but I suspect it's that the fans want to see the singer live the lyrics. To me, that has always explained Judy Garland's appeal and that of Edith Piaf, also. They seemed to bring their pain with them to the performance, like another prop. Pop idols such as Jim Morrison and Johnnie Ray in his early days, brought a blatant, yet sort of innocent, sex appeal to the performance. Billy Idol, on the other hand, and several of the more recent rock stars combine sex with—what seems to me—a dangerous urgency. It's a lot darker in nature.

"I knew Johnnie Ray very well the last few years—the last third, really—of his life and he'd experienced the same thing, and survived it for quite a few more years than Jim managed to, although they had many of the same problems.

"Johnnie and Jim were rather fascinated by each other, but they never did meet. Jim got wasted and died too soon. That fame thing was something they both wanted and courted in the beginning. The last time I saw Jim was about a year before he died. He was drinking away his looks and had gotten involved with some strange witchcraft people. Inadvertently, I think I probably was at least partially responsible for introducing him to that, because I knew this man who claimed to be a witch. Jim was fascinated by that sort of thing and the witch man was fascinated by Jim—most everyone was, then. So I introduced them. The occult was sort of the "in" thing at the time. It was okay to be intellectually interested.

"By that time, Morrison was tired of the fame and the demands, but he was writing some really fine poetry. He wanted to run away from it all, the recording studio, the concerts and just write, but there was no place for him to run to. Johnnie Ray, when he reached that point in the late 1950s, ran off to Spain and lived a couple of years, then eased back into his career in the 1970s. Nevertheless, the old bitch goddess fame was always waiting just around the next corner.

"Toward the end, Johnnie became something of a prisoner in his house on Marmont above Sunset Strip—incidentally, the same general area where Jim lived the last few years. The thing they had in common—and Johnnie came to know that all singers who reach a certain plateau in the public mind have it in common—is that the fans who cheer and scream and become hysterical at a concert are the first to sneer when they see you in public acting human, and make rude comments if you're a little drunk or not dressed to their expectations or whatever.

"I was with Johnnie at a restaurant in West Hollywood in 1988 and we were having a good time because a friend from Australia, a man we were both very fond of, had just flown in. I suppose the conversation was a little loud and, for Johnnie, careless. That ended when a tight-ass couple walked over and told Johnnie he should be ashamed of himself. He was being himself and wasn't living up to their expectations. Now Morrison, on the other hand, invited such treatment and tried to pretend he didn't give a damn, but I always believed he really did.

"Oddly, one of the last serious conversations I had with Johnnie, during the holidays in late 1989, was about this exact thing, and Jim Morrison and Elvis Presley. Of course, Johnnie met Elvis very early on, during his first Las Vegas gig, actually. I have this conversation on tape, because we were working on what was supposed to be John's autobiography, but he was never consistent about that; one day he wanted a book that told everything and the next he didn't want a book at all.

"Johnnie recalled: 'During those days the Vegas hotels staggered the show times and we were able to go to see each other perform. The first night Elvis was in town, he came to see my show and visited backstage with a couple of his people.

"'Later, I went to see his show. Of course, he was in

the process of knocking me off the teen idol perch, but I was five or so years down the road by then and sick to death of it. I had no idea the fans would become such fanatics because I was the first one that had happened to.

'"Backstage, Elvis had about a dozen people surrounding him, a whole gang of his friends and relatives who were all dressed up and trying to look like him. They were all over the place. They had no real function, they were there to share a little reflected adulation, for what that's worth. I never had roadies. The people who traveled with me each had a distinct job to perform and there were never more than three or four of them. Actually, I needed more because I never had a publicity person. I was so Oregon naive that I thought you hired a publicity person to get your name in the papers. And, right from the beginning, I was getting more publicity than Eisenhower and Stalin put together. By the time I learned a publicist's real function was to keep your name out of the scandal sheets, it was too late; the rags had learned they could say anything they wanted about me and no one would do anything about it, because my record company just didn't give a damn. They never thought I'd last more than the next six months, that I was some freak phenomena who would make them some money and be back playing piano lounges for tips again.

'"Elvis had about a dozen people with him and the whole lot was pretty green. And, frankly, they didn't treat me very well. Of course, they did allow him time to have a photo taken with me. It was good publicity for him, then. But I remember leaving there thinking, you poor son of a bitch. Just wait until you get tired of waking up to this day after day. Maybe he finally got so tired of it—got so tired of worrying about whether he could go on another tour, worrying about his weight, getting fat, trying to keep track of all the damn pills—that he really did kill himself.'

"A week or so before Christmas 1989," Locke continues, "I'd stopped by Johnnie's house. He'd been reading Malcolm Forbes' book *They Went That-A-Way* and asked me if I thought there was anything to the report that Morrison had staged his own death as he'd, according to Forbes, often joked about dying. I didn't think so. I don't remember ever hearing Jim talk about death, except one time when he jumped from a second floor balcony into a swimming pool. It was rather dangerous because he had to jump over a concrete strip that was about eight feet wide and someone chided him for being foolish and he made some comment about only having to die once. Supposedly, he'd said he wouldn't mind dying in a plane crash.

"'It would be a good way to go,' is the way it is put in the Malcolm Forbes book. "I just don't want to die of old age or O.D. or drift off in my sleep. I want to feel what it's like. I want to taste it, hear it, smell it. Death is only going to happen once, right? I don't want to miss it.' That certainly sounds like Morrison, but Forbes gave no source reference for the quote. Janis Joplin and Jimi Hendrix both had done drug overdoses a few months before Jim died. Supposedly, after he went to Paris in the spring of 1971 to get away and write poetry, he spent a lot of time drinking, sometimes all night. Forbes stated that, in referring to the drug overdoses of Joplin and Hendrix, he'd say, 'You're drinking with number three.'"

According to his sometime girlfriend Pamela Courson, she and Jim Morrison went out to dinner on Friday, July 2nd, but, after they came home, Jim said he wanted to go out to a movie by himself. Courson said that she woke up about five o'clock the next morning and found Jim lying in a bathtub full of water, dead.

On Monday, July 5th, a representative from Jim's record company, Electra, arrived in the apartment where they'd been staying and found Courson, a sealed coffin and a death certificate stating that Morrison had died of a heart attack. Of course, there was speculation that he'd died of an overdose, as Courson would later do. However, many people who knew Morrison doubted the O.D. theory.

Because of the strange circumstances, his death was not officially confirmed until July 8th. A story quickly spread that Morrison was seen boarding a plane in Paris that weekend and that he'd actually staged his own death. Forbes closed his entry on Morrison by stating that Morrison had gone to Paris to get away from the world of rock 'n roll and to write poetry.

Ray Locke said, "That was exactly what Johnnie asked me about . . . Johnnie was really quite bright, intellectually very curious, and he asked me if I thought there was a chance that Jim Morrison really was still alive. After nearly twenty years? Not a chance in the world. The man had a driven need to be recognized, not so much as a rock 'n roll singer, but as a writer, as Jim Morrison, poet."

In the past, pressure was a fantastic factor on popular singers, even those who surrounded themselves with the best protection that could be bought. Others were offered no protection whatsoever. Billie Holiday, whom Johnnie Ray always credited with being his inspiration and who probably influenced every major singer who came after her, was one who faced the world alone.

Mystique and tragedy surrounded Holiday's personal life. She was so original that no singer ever successfully attempted to copy her style. "There's nobody that can do Billie Holiday. Nobody I ever knew of was foolish enough to try," says Grammy and Tony Award winner Ruth Brown.

Billie was, indeed, an original. Born in Baltimore on April 7, 1915, her entire life alternated between triumph and tragedy. At the age of ten, a neighbor grabbed her and attempted to rape her. She fought back and attracted the police, who took both Billie and her forty-year-old attacker into custody. "They wouldn't let my mother take me home," she recalled later. "They threw me into a cell. My mother cried and screamed and pleaded, but they just put her out of the jailhouse."

When the case came to trial, Billie's assailant was sentenced to five years. Then the judge ordered Billie to be confined to an institution for wayward girls until she reached the age of twenty-one—an eleven year sentence and more than twice that given to the man who tried to rape her. It took two years for her mother to get the judge's ruling reversed. A short while later, Billie was working in a house of prostitution. By the time she was fourteen, she had already served two jail sentences.

When Billie was fifteen, she was auditioning as a dancer, and not doing very well, when a piano player named Dick Wilson asked her if she could sing. She sang "Trav'lin All Alone," a popular song of the time. A speakeasy filled with people quickly grew silent, eyes filled with tears as she held the last notes. People shouted and threw money. She was offered a singing job on the spot. It wasn't long before she moved to a more fashionable club, Monette's, owned by singer Monette Moore. It was there she was discovered by Joe Glaser, Louis Armstrong's manager, and John Hammond, one of the most influential men in jazz music.

At the age of eighteen, she was on her way—to stardom and tragedy. Fame, when it came, struck hard. She recorded "Mean to Me," "My Man," and "I Cried for You," now considered classics. She was sensitive, temperamental and volatile. She became hooked on narcotics early in her career.

Not long after her first recording was cut, Billie was booked into the Apollo Theater, the undisputed zenith for black entertainers. The audiences were tough and they could make or break the career of a newcomer such as Holiday. When she was introduced, she was struck by stage fright and had to be pushed on stage by Pigmeat Markham, a comedian who was also on the bill.

"My knees were shaking so bad the people didn't know whether I was going to dance or sing," Holiday said later. But once she opened her mouth, she grew confident and the audience became still. "They didn't ask me what my style was (or) where I came from, who influenced me or anything. They just broke up the place," she said later. Before her week-long engagement was up, Ralph Schiffman, who owned the Apollo, had booked her for a return engagement in August.

That summer, John Hammond got together some of the best jazz musicians and put them into a recording studio with Billie. The brilliant piano man, Teddy Wilson, trumpeter Roy Eldridge, and saxophonist Ben Webster were among the musicians she recorded with that first year. They were paid very little, but those John Hammond produced sides are now considered some of the best jazz recordings ever made.

In saxophone player Lester Young Billie found a soul mate. They became lovers and, in that summer of 1937, recorded "I Must Have that Man" and "Sun Showers" together. He nicknamed her "Lady Day" and she called him "The President," or "Pres," the king of the sax players. To them, the nicknames were just a way of having fun, but both have lasted over the years.

Billie was doing dope with Young and, by the time she got a job making her first big money—$14 a day—by going on the road with the Count Basie Orchestra, she was hooked. Young was also in the band, but it was John Hammond who convinced Basie he needed a "girl singer." It was a time of racial taboos and, in Detroit, the management of the Fix Theater told Billie she was "too light" to be singing with a negro band and insisted she darken her complexion with makeup.

After eight months of touring, Holiday quit the Basie band. There were rumors she was fired because of her narcotics problem. She immediately joined the Artie Shaw band, an all-white group. The integrated band was viewed by many with suspicion. Once, in the south, the band members painted a red dot on her forehead and checked her into a hotel as an "Indian Princess."

On December 28, 1938, Billie got her biggest break—the opening of the Cafe Society in Greenwich Village. The club and Billie Holiday were a hit from the first night. It was there that poet Lewis Allen gave her the words to "Strange Fruit," a protest against racism. The words "strange fruit" refer to the bodies of lynched blacks hanging from the branches of a tree. With the help of accompanist Sonny White, Billie adapted it to music and the song became a sensation. In spite of the slow, dramatic style of the song—a different pace for Billie—the recording made her a celebrity. For the next few years, her star grew, especially after she recorded another song she co-wrote, "God Bless the Child."

However, the use of opiates, which had started out as a lark, influenced her choice of a first husband. She married Jimmy Monroe on August 25, 1941 and immediately began sharing his opium pipe.

By the time she moved to Decca Records in 1944, her narcotics usage had become serious. But, outside of the music world which tended to look the other way, it was still secret. Billie changed to Decca to work with her friend Milt Gabler, who had recorded "Strange Fruit," and because she would be allowed to experiment more on her recordings there. The first recording at Decca introduced an innovation in jazz; "Lover Man" utilized a strong section.

"Jimmy (Monroe) was no more the cause of doing what I did than my mother was. That goes for any man I ever knew. I was as strong, if not stronger, than any of them." Holiday was talking about her use of heroin, which, by the beginning of 1947, had gotten such a grip on her that even she knew something had to be done.

She sought help, checked into a New York sanitarium and went "cold turkey." Unfortunately, the news alerted agents of the United States Bureau of Narcotics and several were assigned to watch her. While she was appearing at the Earle Theater in Philadelphia on May 16th, agents raided her hotel room. She fled with a trumpet player with whom she was having an affair. A few days later, they were arrested in a hotel room and rushed to trial one week later. In the hopes that she would be placed in the rehabilitation center in Lexington, Kentucky, Billie pleased guilty. Instead she was sentenced to one year and a day at the Federal Women's Reformatory at Alderson, West Virginia.

Released early for good behavior, Billie was back in New York the following March but soon faced another disappointment: because of her narcotics conviction, she could not get a cabaret permit to play nightclubs. But she could play Carnegie Hall and was booked there for a concert on March 27, 1948. She looked and sounded better than she had in years and got several standing ovations from the full house.

Actually that Easter Eve concert was the highpoint of Billie's career. Several successful Broadway theater engagements followed, but the drug label stuck. Agents and local police constantly harassed her.

Worse still, she signed on with a man named John Levy as her manager and apparently also became his lover and often referred to him as "my husband."

Levy was one of the worst things that ever happened to her; not only did he steal most of the money Billie made that year—and she worked constantly—he also caused her to get busted in San Francisco in January, 1949. Having been warned shortly before police entered their hotel room, Levy handed Billie the narcotics and fled. She was charged but underwent tests to prove she was not on drugs.

She was exonerated but barely had enough money to pay her legal fees. Alone again, she turned to heroin to deal with her insecurities. In 1951 she signed with Norman Granz. Holiday was only happy when she was working so Granz kept her working steadily for the next five years. She re-recorded many of her old songs, and dozens of new ones. A 1954 European tour was a sensation; she played to a crowd of 6,000 at London's Royal Albert Hall. "It was the thrill of my life," she said later.

"It certainly was the thrill of my life," Johnnie Ray said in an interview. "Although she had come to see me perform twice that I knew of, that was the first time I saw her live. The next time I saw her was not such a happy occasion. She was playing a little bar on Hollywood Boulevard and it was toward the end. I don't think there was much publicity, if any, much note taken that the great Billie Holiday was playing a bar in Hollywood. But I tried to keep track of her because she was not only my inspiration, I adored her immediately when I met her the first time, in Detroit, in 1951. Some musicians told me she was playing the place in Hollywood—I think it was The Seven Seas—and I went to see her. She was as great as ever and the hardcore fans were there. A year or so later she was gone."

Gone, indeed. Lady Day collapsed while playing a small Greenwich Village club on May 25, 1959. A week later she lapsed into a coma and was admitted to a city hospital because she was broke. She was suffering from cirrhosis and heart disease. But life wasn't quite through with her. On June 12 police arrested her in her hospital bed for drug possession. A nurse said she had found some white powder wrapped in foil nearby. Billie Holiday never left the hospital and died on July 17. The nurses found a fifty dollar bill taped to one of her legs.

Janis Joplin and Jimi Hendrix lived hard and died young within two-and-a-half weeks of one another. Hendrix was a sensation in the late 1960s, best known now for his recordings of "Purple Haze," "Foxy Lady," and his off-beat guitar version of "The Star Spangled Banner." In life—and unfortunately there is very little film of his performances—he was equally as well-known for his wild stage antics. He played guitars on his back, between his legs, with his teeth, and usually in time to his gyrating hips. It was a stoned era and Jimi was the most stoned of them all. He popped pills by the bottle and would open his mouth to accept unidentified drugs from the members of his audiences.

By mid-1970, when he was twenty-seven, the drugs and fast life began to affect his performances. He was booed at concerts, and at New York's Madison Square Garden, he threw his guitar to the stage and stalked off, saying, "I just can't get it together."

Apparently he anticipated his death because not long before it came, he said, "I tell you when I die I'm not going to have a funeral. I'm going to have a jam session. And knowing me, I'll probably get busted at my own funeral."

He was sleeping with Monika Danneman, Mick Jagger's former girlfriend, when death came on September 18, 1970. Danneman said later that she had taken a sleeping pill out of a package containing ten. Hendrix took the other nine. That was about seven o'clock in the morning. When Danneman awoke about three-and-a-half hours later, Hendrix had vomited in his sleep. When she couldn't awaken him she called for an ambulance. Jimi Hendrix died soon after he arrived at a nearby hospital. He had suffocated in his own vomit.

Perhaps his death was accidental, but many people believed at the time that Hendrix killed himself. His career had recently taken a nose dive that was as speedy as had been his rise to fame. He was buried in Seattle beneath a seven-foot-long flower arrangement in the shape of a guitar. His musician friends did, indeed, hold a jam session at the grave. And *Newsweek* magazine asked, "Who's next?"

The answer came two-and-a-half weeks later—Janis Joplin. She was already twenty-three when she arrived in San Francisco from the Texas gulf coast town of Port Arthur in 1966. The "hippy, flower-child" culture was just beginning and Janis had an uneasy feeling that it was quickly passing her by. She was in a hurry. "I won't last as long as other singers, maybe. But I think you can destroy your now by worrying about tomorrow."

She didn't waste a lot of time but, of course, did worry about tomorrow. Within a year she had put together the best blues/rock bands of the era. And it did not "just happen" as she had claimed in an interview. She had been listening to, and singing along with, black blues singers for most of her life. And by the time she was in high school she had a pretty good idea of what she was going to do with her short life.

A year after her San Francisco move she walked off
with the 1967 Monterrey Rock Festival. Janis was ready
and Janis was what was happening.

And Janis told people that she wouldn't live past the
age of thirty. And Janis believed it.

Janis told people she had been voted the ugliest
freshman boy at the University of Texas. And people believed her. She asked the makers of Southern Comfort for
a fur coat because she chug-a-lugged a bottle of their
whisky onstage at every performance. She didn't need the
coat or, according to a friend at the time, particularly want
it. She wanted to make them give it to her. It was a power
trip.

She did drugs and, like Billie Holiday, heroin was her
drug of choice. She was tugged and pulled here and there
by her fans and by the press. She actually enjoyed the
press attention and loved making up bizarre stories just to
see if the tales would be printed.

Then Janis went to Los Angeles in the fall of 1970 to
work on a new album. She checked into the Landmark
Hotel in the heart of Hollywood. It was near a source of
heroin, and only about three blocks from the bar where
Billie Holiday had last played in the place called "the cruel
city."

She got her supply of heroin. On the evening of October 3, Janis worked on the new album at a nearby sound
studio. Afterward, she went out for a few drinks with
friends. She returned to the hotel about midnight, got
change for cigarettes from the hotel clerk, and went to her
room. She shot up with the new supply of white stuff. It
was said she died about 1:40 on Sunday morning, somewhat over an hour after buying cigarettes. Late the next
day her guitarist became worried and had the hotel per-
sonnel open her door. Janis, who gave her all at every performance, had given her last.

Some people believe she killed herself. There were
rumors of trouble with a new boyfriend, but, an overdose is
an overdose.

Amphetamines and alcohol are a volatile mixture, and Judy Garland developed a problem with both while under contract to MGM. She started taking "diet pills" (which were nothing more than amphetamines) in an effort to lose weight when she was no more than a child. Everyone in Hollywood knew about Judy's pill and booze problem, including the head of MGM, Louis B. Mayer. Certainly the Hollywood press knew that little Judy had serious problems, and many knew the very nature of those problems early on. By the time she was seventeen she was seeing a psychiatrist.

Judy's life was like a roller coaster ride. One year she would be down, couldn't find a job, divorcing a husband, or marrying a new one; the very next year she would be back on top—sometimes even happily married.

However, once she left the protective arm of MGM—no matter how much money she had made for the studio—Judy was on her own. It didn't take long for her pill and booze inspired escapades to begin making headlines. As an independent singer, no matter how big her star, she no longer enjoyed a buffer between herself and the press—and her public, for that matter.

Without a studio contract, Judy was just another singer, as far as the press was concerned. And singers were the most vulnerable targets around. They always were and still are. Again, this is probably because they so intimately touch their audiences, since there is no wall between a singer and the audience, no army of technicians performing miracles with the film and on the soundtrack. Until certain rock stars started lip-syncing their concerts, a singer's performance was a one-on-one affair between the performer and each member of the audience. A movie star could go through an entire career without ever interacting with the audience, or ever seeing a member of the press except under the most controlled conditions. Singers never had that luxury.

Ray Locke remembers that, in 1969, Johnnie Ray was in England when Garland came there for a club date. Accompanying Judy was Mickey Deans, the thirty-five year old former manager of the New York discotheque, Arthur's. She was wined, dined, and lauded for her first London engagement in several years. Sadly, once the engagement was over, Judy had no place to go. The Internal Revenue Service was on her back in the States and she had no forthcoming job offers.

"Judy and Mickey Deans moved into Johnnie Ray's London house. 'It was difficult,' Johnnie recalled. 'They fought constantly, then they got married and things only got worse. I was the best man at their wedding. Poor Judy. She invited the press and everyone she knew in London, and that was a lot of people. None of them showed up. The press barely showed up because Judy was old news. It was really very sad.

'Then Bill Franklin, who was managing me at the time, saw that I was going crazy dealing with Judy and Deans. He thought of the idea of our Scandinavian concert tour. She was in top form. We played Stockholm, Copenhagen, four or five cities, and she was only late once and that time she was really ill. We had offers to take the show all over, Germany, France, Japan. But I had an Australian booking to play off, several weeks. And I didn't want to leave Judy and Deans in my house so I went and paid the rent for the mews house where she died. I played my Australian dates and was on my way back to London with a stop in California.

'"I fell into bed exhausted at home in Malibu, when we arrived Saturday, June 21, 1969. Early the next morning the telephone rang. Judy was dead."'

Judy Garland's every false move, every loud drinking bout, every shouting match with her husband, former husband, or husband-to-be was headlined around the world. Judy was good copy once she left MGM but she couldn't get the "A" press to show up for her last wedding. It took her death of "an incautious self-over-dosage of sleeping pills" to get that kind of attention again.

In the 1940s, Frank Sinatra was the idol of millions. Women screamed and fainted at the sight of him. His recordings out-sold those of any pop singer that came before him. His popular music rivals were Tony Bennett, Doris Day, Peggy Lee and Dinah Shore—all band singers at the end of the "big band" era. But Frank was what was happening, he was the one the fans screamed for. No one knows exactly why his career—and his personal life—began to go wrong in the late 40s.

There was probably no one factor that led to his fall from popularity—and the pop charts—in the late 40s and early 50s. It would appear that there were several contributing factors. The public's musical taste was being influenced by country singers and black blues singers who had "crossed over" to a white audience. And, Sinatra's recordings from this period sound hurried. He had become a bit temperamental and was often short with club owners, bookers, and musicians. He had also long since grown tired of the press following him around. By 1950 he was washed up professionally, and his storybook marriage to his childhood sweetheart, Nancy, was over. He hit the front pages once he started openly dating—and living with—Ava Gardner.

He had broken too many of the "rules." He had always been a womanizer but he was a family man with three children, and a Roman Catholic. Leaving his faithful Italian wife for the sexy screen siren caused the press and the public to turn on him. A supposedly indignant press corps went for the jugular. Sinatra had never endeared himself to them and perhaps this was seen as a way to get back at him.

In May 1950 Nancy Sinatra's attorneys announced she was filing for divorce. What the press didn't announce—and they knew it—was that while Nancy was giving up Frank, she was in turn taking just about every dime he had.

Later that year Ava and Frank, very much in love, wed. With the release of both *Pandora and the Flying*

Dutchman and *Showboat* that year, Ava became a major MGM star; Sinatra was reduced to playing what he'd later himself describe as "joints." Ava showed up to see him in one of these places just once. The audience ignored his onstage singing and began shouting "Ava! Ava! Ava!" Sinatra walked off the stage.

Certainly they were in love and certainly they were extremely jealous of each other. Their fights became legendary. One such fight at their Palm Springs house involved Lana Turner and furnished material for the scandal sheets for years.

The stories and scandal hurt Ava but she never let it show. A shoot-from-the-hip type from North Carolina, Gardner was painfully honest and liked by everyone. Those legendary public—and private—battles between the Sinatras, however, ended up as fodder for the media—along with the idea that he was always the heavy. They jumped all over him when he was down, so who can blame him for his later distrust of the press. Not I. To this day his relationship with the media—and he has long had some of the most efficient press relations people in the business working for him—is tenuous at best.

CHAPTER 9

Marilyn and Her Sisters

Marilyn Monroe was the ultimate movie star, the world's sex goddess supreme.

It has been almost thirty years since, on Sunday, August 5, 1962, Dr. Hyman Engleberg called the Los Angeles police department at 4:25 a.m. to report that she was dead, but the memory of a woman, obsessed by a tragic dream, lingers.

She was *Playboy's* first "Playmate," but, two years before, when it was leaked to the press that she had posed for a nude calendar while a struggling young actress in 1949, the studio heads held their collective breath, but quickly recovered when they realized that the leak had not damaged her career. One, according to Norman Mailer in his biography *Marilyn*, even asked her such personal questions as to whether her asshole was showing in the photograph, whether she had spread her legs, or whether there were any animals in the picture with her.

In those days, movie stars did not pose nude, but Marilyn had. Much to the delight of her male fans—and probably to the secret admiration of many women—she refused to deny it. When studio executives saw that the public was not going to turn on her in moral indignation, they bought up copies of the calendar and gave them to members of the press as a promotional gimmick.

Marilyn, after all, was an orphan—or so everyone thought at the time. She had grown up in foster homes, the epitome of the underdog who had made good. Americans

151

have always been inordinately fond of underdogs, and Marilyn had other things going for her: that walk, the little girl voice, the blonde hair and that body.

Marilyn cleverly manipulated the image, relating her horror stories to the press about her childhood: she had been raped "seven or eight times" before she was twelve; she was a poor orphan who had been forced to wear hideous uniforms and clean out toilets; and her mother was long dead.

None of it was true.

But it didn't really matter if her mother was alive or if the people who had raised her were salt-of-the-earth, middle-class Americans who claimed her horror stories were not true. The public believed what they wanted to—and forgave her the rest.

Marilyn Monroe was born Norma Jean Baker in the maternity ward of Los Angeles General Hospital on June 1, 1926. Her mother, Gladys Monroe Baker, was a film cutter at Consolidated Film Industries. Her father, according to biographer Fred Guiles, was C. Stanley Gifford, who apparently loved Gladys, but deserted her.

Unable to care for the child herself, Gladys boarded Norma Jean with a Hawthorne, California family named Bolender, who lived across the street from Gladys' parents. Both of Gladys' parents would spend their last years in a sanatorium. Contrary to Marilyn's press revelations, Albert Bolender, a mail carrier, and his family treated her kindly, as they did their other foster children.

When Norma Jean was six, Gladys bought a small house in Hollywood and took her daughter to live with her. Soon afterward, however, she was committed after a breakdown and Norma Jean's future was left in the hands of a family friend, Grace McKee. Although Grace would continue to look after Norma Jean's interests until her first marriage, she was initially forced to place her into the Los Angeles Orphans Home and later with foster parents.

Later, Marilyn would tell reporters that she had been mistreated in the home, forced to "wash a hundred plates, a hundred cups, a hundred knives, forks and spoons three times a day, seven days a week, scrub toilets and bathtubs."

"She never washed any dishes and she never scrubbed toilets," the orphanage superintendent would tell Maurice Zolotow years later. "The most she ever did was help dry the dishes one hour a week. One hour, that's all."

Marilyn would say that she was in seven or eight foster homes following the orphanage, raped before she reached the age of nine, forced to scrub floors, made to take her bath in dirty water that had been used by others, made to sleep in a closet without windows and was subjected to rapes by old men.

Actually, she had only two foster homes after leaving the orphanage at the age of eleven and then went to live with Grace McKee in Van Nuys, where she attended Emerson Junior High School and Van Nuys High. She quit school in February, 1942, and married Jim Dougherty that June.

Jim Dougherty says that Norma Jean was a virgin when he married her.

But the stories made good copy, and Marilyn Monroe knew their worth from the beginning. She and the press had an unspoken pact.

The marriage lasted until October, 1946, when Marilyn, now modeling under the name of Jean Norman, flew to Reno and divorced Dougherty. Earlier that year, she had been on a tour of the West with photographer Andre de Dienes, who photographed her fresh-faced, innocent, and clean-scrubbed, with kinky brown hair. When de Dienes, the first of many lovers, asked to photograph her nude, Marilyn refused, stating, "Don't you understand? I'm going to be a great movie star some day."

Marilyn's photograph appeared on the covers of *Laff and Peek*, *U.S. Camera*, *Parade* and *Pageant*. When Emmeline Snively, the owner of Marilyn's modeling agency, concocted a story about an interest in Marilyn on the part of Howard Hughes, it was enough to get her a screen test at Twentieth Century-Fox. Three days after the test, they signed her to a contract. After bits in films like *Scudda Hoo! Scudda Hay!*, they dropped her option and Columbia Pictures signed her.

Columbia used her in one picture, *Ladies of the Chorus*, but were no more impressed with her talents than Twentieth Century-Fox. They also dropped her. At this point, Marilyn, needing money to make her car payment, accepted photographer Tom Kelley's offer of fifty dollars to pose nude for the calendar that would catapult her to fame three years later.

A bit in a Marx Brothers comedy, *Love Happy*, brought Marilyn to the attention of one of Hollywood's top agents, Johnny Hyde. Hyde fell in love with her, leaving his wife and family, and managed to get her another contract with Fox.

Her studio rushed her into several films to capitalize on her popularity: *Hometown Girl* (on loan-out to Metro-Goldwyn-Mayer), *As Young As You Feel, Love Nest, We're Not Married, O'Henry's Full House* and *River of No Return*. But her initial mediocre movies masked a talent that would surface only in her later movies. Hollywood was not impressed with Marilyn, but the press and movie audiences were beginning to pay attention. Her appearance in *Asphalt Jungle* pushed her over the edge and she became a name to contend with by the time the studio loaned her out for a featured role in Fritz Lang's *Clash By Night* with Barbara Stanwyck, Robert Ryan and Paul Douglas. In an interview, Stanwyck predicted that "In a few years, we'll be supporting her in pictures."

It didn't take long. A few months later, she was a star in *Don't Bother To Knock* and, when Jerry Wald found out about the nude calendar and leaked it to the press, she became a star.

Two years later, Marilyn married America's hero Joe DiMaggio after a long and well-publicized courtship. The marriage was stormy from the beginning. DiMaggio apparently wanted a wife, but had married a love goddess. He also had a wife with a history of using the drug Seconal.

During the filming of *There's No Business Like Show Business*, Marilyn was constantly ill and drinking a great deal. By the time her next film, *The Seven Year Itch*, was finished filming in New York, Marilyn announced that she and DiMaggio were parting.

Separated from her husband, Marilyn rebelled against her studio, moved to New York and formed a company to produce her own films with Milton Greene. After frantic attempts to replace her with other stars, Fox gave in to her demands and she returned to make *Bus Stop*. The studio had given her more money, plus cast, director and script approval. But they still had the old Marilyn. Much to their dismay, she had replaced her former coach with Paula Strasberg, and insisted that Strasberg have the final approval on all scenes. She became more tardy and more temperamental than ever. However, the film was extremely popular and made money.

Next came *Some Like It Hot*.

Director Billy Wilder has declared that Marilyn almost drove him crazy on the set of *Some Like It Hot*. She was subject to lateness, some days as much as six hours, while Wilder and co-stars Jack Lemmon, Tony Curtis and Joe E. Brown stood around. When she did arrive on the set, it often took as many as forty-seven takes to get three words of Monroe dialogue on film. Tony Curtis, sweating in heavy makeup and drag, stated that acting with Monroe was like "kissing Hitler."

After the filming, Wilder admitted to a reporter that he was hardly able to "look at my wife without wanting to hit her because she is a woman." When Marilyn's husband, Arthur Miller, sent the director a telegram protesting that Marilyn was the "salt of the earth," the director replied that the "salt of the earth" had told his assistant director "to go fuck himself."

Some Like It Hot remains one of Marilyn Monroe's best films.

Marrying Arthur Miller on June 29, 1956, Marilyn spent her honeymoon making *The Prince and the Showgirl*.

She became pregnant, but suffered a miscarriage and spent months recovering. While she recuperated, Arthur Miller started writing *The Misfits* for her.

The Misfits was shot in Nevada. Conditions were uncomfortable and hot, with Clark Gable, Montogomery Clift and other stars waiting patiently under the hot sun for Marilyn to arrive. Marilyn had already had her well-publicized affair with Yves Montand during the filming of *Let's Make Love* and her behavior on the set was erratic. She became highly addicted to Nembutals. The filming was finally concluded, but in the weeks after the shooting, Clark Gable suffered a massive heart attack and died. Marilyn returned to New York and announced she was divorcing Miller. At the same time, she learned that Yves Montand was returning to his wife, Simone Signoret.

That winter, Marilyn ended up in Payne-Whitney, a hospital for mental disorders. DiMaggio came to her rescue and had her transferred to Columbia-Presbyterian, from which she was released three weeks later, only to read that Kay Gable, Clark's widow, had stated that she believed Marilyn's conduct during *The Misfits* had brought on her husband's fatal heart attack.

Marilyn attempted suicide, but was saved. Friends convinced her to move back to California and she purchased a house at 12305 Fifth Helena Drive in Brentwood. She began work on *Something's Got to Give*. Gossip linked her with Frank Sinatra, Robert Kennedy and even President John F. Kennedy when she defied her studio bosses to fly to New York to sing "Happy Birthday" at his Madison Square Garden party.

Returning to Hollywood, Marilyn seldom showed up for work, giving illness as an excuse. When she did report, she was seldom in the mood to work.

Whether by accident or suicide (and there have also been dark wispers of murder), Marilyn died that night in August 1962 . . . but the legend grows. The Marilyn Monroe business is booming. Department and gift stores sell Marilyn Monroe dolls, jigsaw puzzles, playing cards, date books, wall posters, and calendars.

She is hard to forget.

"How do you get to meet Jayne Mansfield?"

"Buy a camera."

Publicity-shy she was not. Jayne Mansfield, nee Vera Jayne Palmer from Bryn Mawr, Pennsylvania, was born on April 19, 1933, married at sixteen, a mother at seventeen. When she and her husband moved to Los Angeles, she studied at the University of California and tried to break into movies.

She finally was included in a group of starlets sent to Florida to publicize a Jane Russell movie *Underwater*. Her 40-22-35 figure drew most of the attention and resulted in a number of minor film roles. In an effort to boost her career, Jayne looked for a Broadway play and found it in *Will Success Spoil Rock Hunter*. Her scene played wrapped only in a bath towel made not only Broadway notice her, but Hollywood as well. She played against the usual Broadway to Hollywood scenario and was allowed to play the same role in the film version, and followed it with roles in *The Wayward Bus* with Dan Dailey and *Kiss Them For Me* with Cary Grant. But then her career took a monotonous turn; she played major parts in minor movies or minor parts in major movies. Eventually, she was offered quickie films, or exploitive films in which she appeared nude or semi-nude.

But, although the studios ignored her, the public and media did not. She was sought after for personal appearances and went with Bob Hope on three of his overseas tours to entertain servicemen. Always willing to step onto a stage, she was also well groomed, showing generous cleavage, smiling and throwing kisses. She was one star who was always on time.

Almost entirely due to the media and her own invention, Jayne Mansfield became an international sex star. This blonde blend of bosomy sex and press agentry lived in a thirty-five room pink mansion and was presented to the

Queen of England. She was successful on stage, in films, and in nightclubs and dinner theaters throughout the country.

Her trials and exploits became media events: being mobbed in Paris, robbed in Las Vegas, disrobed by Mardi Gras crowds in Rio de Janeiro and lost in the Caribbean. On stage and in public she had countless mishaps, mostly involving broken straps and dysfunctioning zippers.

People laughed, but not unkindly. Jayne Mansfield had become a joke, but she was laughing along with the rest. She continued performing and pleasing crowds.

Jayne Mansfield finished her nightclub act in Biloxi, Mississippi at 2:25 a.m. on June 29, 1967, and was being driven to New Orleans—a two hour drive—for a television appearance. With her was Sam Brody and three of her five children: Maria, Zoltan and Mickey, Jr. The car was driven by a twenty-year-old pre-law student from the University of Mississippi who knew the road very well.

The three adults sat in the front seat and the children were asleep in the back seat.

In the suburbs of New Orleans, city crews had been spraying insecticide mist into the air to kill mosquitoes. A truck-trailer rig had slowed down on a curve on U.S. 90 known as The Spanish Trail because of decreased visibility. The car in which Jayne Mansfield and her children were being driven came around the curve at high speed and struck the back of the trailer with such force that the top of the auto was sheared back, killing the three adults instantly. Jayne Mansfield was decapitated. The children escaped with relatively minor injuries.

The news of Jayne's death brought sorrow to the Hollywood community. She had been liked and respected as a basically nice person, and a devoted mother, who pursued her own version of the American Dream with all her strength in the only way she knew how.

Mansfield's first husband was Paul Mansfield, whom she married in 1950. They had one child, Jayne Marie, and were divorced in 1957. In 1958, she married Mickey Hargitay and moved into the pink mansion at 10100 Sunset Boulevard with its heart-shaped pool and ankle-deep white carpeting. They had three children and divorced in 1963. In 1964, she tried marriage for the third time with director Matt Cimber. They had one child, Antonio—only twenty months old at the time of her death—but were separated at the time of her death.

She had been seeing Sam Brody for about a year. Brody, a Los Angeles attorney, had been sued for divorce on the grounds of adultery in 1967, named Jayne Mansfield in her petition. Brody was a gambler who was in debt at the time of the accident. Jayne's busy schedule was an attempt to help him financially.

You could find Inger Stevens at a crowded party just by cocking your ear and listening for her distinct laughter, which was throaty and contagious. A healthy, vibrant, intelligent actress and woman who had already one extremely successful television series, "The Farmer's Daughter," and several movies behind her, she was preparing to begin production on another.

At the age of thirty-five, on April 30, 1970, Inger Stevens was found dead in the kitchen of her Woodrow Wilson house by a woman, part of a film crew, whom she had allowed to live in part of her house, since Inger and her husband mainly lived in another house by the Pacific Ocean. The official reason for her death was acute barbituate intoxication.

Was it suicide . . .accident? Who was Inger Stevens? A few intimate friends in her life knew her as a woman with strong feelings and an appetitie for life, with political awareness (she knew Robert Kennedy and Hubert Humphrey, both of whom were presented with lists of urgent societal problems *and* Inger's ideas for solutions, be it education or prison reform or whatever), and a deep commitment to her work with abused and disturbed children, as well as being a dedicated actress.

A coroner's conclusion, based on a psychological autopsy, took a different approach as have many writers when they sketch a sad, lonely figure, a "hard luck girl," never neglecting to mention that she had attempted suicide once before.

Born in Sweden on October 18, 1934, Inger experienced her parents' divorce when she was five. She was raised by an aunt, and it took years before she understood why her mother, who had seven children in all, could not cope. When she was twelve, her father, a professor who had moved to America and remarried, sent for her and her younger brother. The two scared kids traveled across the Atlantic on a freighter and arrived in a strange country where a man said to Inger, "You're a foreigner, aren't you?" How did he know? "Your shoes!" She went home and burned the shoes, for which she got into trouble.

Inger and her stepmother did not get along. At sixteen, she ran away from home and worked in a burlesque show in Kansas City. "Sweet sixteen? No, difficult confused sixteen," said she who told about this experience so one could see the dilapidated house, the skinny girl with clenched teeth who climbed steep, dark stairs, humming to keep her fears at bay. From the ad she believed the job was to sell popcorn and take tickets. She entered a room and a cigar-chewing man studied her. "Can you dance?" She knew folk dancing and the waltz and . . . "Sixty-five dollars a week if you dance," the man said, handing her a shiny blue dress with a deep neckline. She had a job in the show *Blue Champagne*. The next few evenings turned into a nightmare for the young girl. Would the police discover she was underage? How could she avoid men stinking of cheap liquor who seemed to have hands everywhere? She hoped her father would come but pride forbade her to call him.

Eventually, her father did come. She returned home and graduated from high school. After graduation, she went to New York, worked as a chorus girl, did commercials and took acting lessons. At age twenty, she married her agent, but the marriage only lasted four months, although she would continue to pay alimony to him for years. Work in the theater, television and, when she was twenty-four, a leading movie role opposite Bing Crosby in *Man On Fire* moved her career steadily forward.

In 1958, she fell in love with a married man, a talented entertainer, who, after a year of bliss, decided to return to his wife. In a moment of despair and loneliness, Inger attempted to take her life but was discovered in time and saved. Later she would comment, "If I had broken my leg on New Year's Eve 1959, people would expect it to be healed by now. I broke my heart and impulsively did something stupid. Now I'm older, wiser and healed. Why must they always drag up that incident?"

Then, at a party she met Ike Jones. Books and articles have called him "a black musician" but, sorry to say, he is not exceptionally musical! A former UCLA football star with a degree in business administration, Jones was Nat King Cole's producer when he met Inger Stevens. Later Inger and he were partners/owners of a chain of convalescent homes, and his business acumen was invaluable to her.

The two fell in love and were secretly married in Mexico on November 18, 1961.

At the time, Inger was starring in the popular television series "The Farmer's Daughter." She and Ike faced the dilemma that should they openly declare their marriage, Inger's career would be ruined, according to all experts. Audiences of the early sixties were not ready to accept a case of miscegenation. The alternative was for Ike to remain "hidden." Inger leaned toward openness, whatever the cost, but Ike opted for secrecy, unable to accept the responsibility of destroying her hard-won career.

The situation created a tremendous strain on their relationship. Handsome, intelligent, charming, and unofficially a "single man," Ike attracted women, and he strayed from a monogamous path. Inger, with wounded pride and aching heart, understood psychologically and intellectually. "What is this doing to him, to be hidden, to pretend, not even to be able to drive my car if his is at the shop, to evade journalists, to read about my pretend-dates for publicity's sake, to go out for dinner and always bring someone else along so it won't be obvious that he is with me? When will this idiocy and bigotry end? Am I a coward? Is my career more important to me than Ike? I try to make it up to him in other ways, but is it enough? Sometimes it would be so much easier not to be with Ike, to be with a guy with the accepted skin color . . . But I love him! They are not going to get to us! We'll win! Because it's just stupidity and ignorance. And you know, a career can't put its arms around you and hug you hard. Things are so good between us, most of the time . . ."

There were times though when emotion won over intellect and Inger tried to even the score by doing to him what he did to her.

It was a stormy marriage at times, but it remained a strong union as the two always found their way back to each other. Their greatest marital crisis came in 1968 when they lived apart for three months. Inger said she wanted a divorce, but couldn't find the marriage certificate when she was ready to see the lawyer. She burst out laughing, realizing that she had only wanted a break so that they could start over again.

Every bit of unhappiness in their marriage cannot be blamed on racial attitudes. The two were also strong, stubborn, vulnerable individuals, each with scars from the past. But they were dealing with their lives and working things out. Inger had been talking regularly to a psychiatrist (actually two—but the first one fell in love with her during their fifth session and she ended that relationship). "We are on our way toward rather absolute honesty," she said about six weeks before her death.

At the time of her death, she had made several decisions. She would make a new, big television series to firmly establish herself and make a considerable amount of money. After that she would put her private life and happiness first. "And if nobody wants to employ me, we'll make our own movies!" Both she and Ike wanted to have a baby. His management of their business was making them financially independent. Both could see signs of attitudes slowly changing and looked forward to black and white being purely descriptive words.

Then the actress with the sky-blue eyes, whose freckles formed a bridge when she wrinkled her nose in laughter, was found on an April morning, lying face down on her kitchen floor, having ingested a number of sleeping pills. Ike was at their other home—she had stayed at the house in town due to early morning appointments in preparation for the series.

"Who through every inch of his life weaves a pattern of vigor and elation can never taste death but goes to sleep among the stars." So wrote one of Inger's favorite writers, Irish Sean O'Casey. A fitting epitaph. Much more so than the "poor sad girl" variations. Though, in retrospect, the painful truth is that Inger Stevens was too honest, too full of love and ready to give it, too sensitive and too decent to understand or cope with a world that is frequently suspicious, hard and murderous on those who are vulnerable and willing to expose themselves. There were good, supportive people in Hollywood, and yet the society at large was harsh enough not to let her publicly and proudly acknowledge the man she loved without risking her whole career. Had she had just a bit of the toughness that characterizes those of us who "make it," she might have survived.

One of the most beautiful of the tragic blondes of Hollywood came from Texas in 1945 and began a life that was to read like a sordid "B" film. Barbara Payton's young, Air Force captain groom, John Payton, was tall, handsome and everything a seventeen-year-old girl could want. They came to Hollywood for their honeymoon and stayed at the Knickerbocker Hotel near Hollywood and Vine. But Barbara was beautiful and ambitious:

"That Hollywood honeymoon was the first step to the end of our marriage. It made no sense. Why should I be married to just one man, have a dull life and raise a family, when I could have all that glamour?"

Barbara met an agent and talent scout for a major studio at poolside, who offered to help her in films. But she had one major problem:

"Pregnancy! I was so damn mad at John that I ordered him out of the house. He had to go back to camp anyway."

Pregnancy—and being alone in Hollywood—didn't faze Barbara. She had already made up her mind to take the agent's offer. She filed for divorce and went home to Texas, where she gave birth to her son—whom she left to be reared by her parents. She returned to California and, by the end of the first year, was named as one of the "Baby Stars" most likely to succeed, taking her place beside Piper Laurie, Mona Freeman, Debbie Reynolds, Mala Powers and Barbara Bates.

Within the year, she was dating sophisticated Franchot Tone and had her first major role in *Trapped* with Lloyd Bridges. From there, she went into *Kiss Tomorrow Goodbye* with James Cagney. Her career was off to a fast start.

Beautiful—and hungry for recognition—Barbara used every device in her power, including a sensational body and a willing disposition toward anyone who could help her career.

In the next few years, Hollywood media found her love life much more interesting than her screen life. Her indecision regarding two men, Tone and actor Tom Neal, made tabloid headlines again and again. For a time, she had affairs with both, then married Tone, divorced him, married Neal, but continued to date Tone. Finally, she divorced Neal and continued to play the entire field.

Meanwhile, her small studio, Eagle-Lion, was making a profit loaning her out to other studios. More interested in profit than quality, the studio action resulted in a string of rather bland films, even though they pitted Barbara against some well-known star attractions: Guy Madison in *Drums in the Deep South*, Gregory Peck in *Only the Valiant*, and Gary Cooper in *Dallas*.

But Barbara was making $10,000 a week and loved to party every night. She began to gain weight and lose her looks. By the mid-1950s, the movie offers stopped. She began "borrowing" money from men she dated. Finally, one of them set her straight: "Barbara, you go to bed with every man you date and ask him to lend you money. You're a hooker."

She was arrested several times for shoplifting and being drunk and disorderly. But, only eleven years after the peak of her Hollywood career, she was arrested for hustling on Hollywood Boulevard. Media described her as overweight, bloated and scarred from being attacked by one of her johns. Her price was five dollars a trick.

In her 1963 autobiography, *I'm Not Ashamed*, Barbara described her "B" picture existence: "I live in a rat-roach infested apartment with not a bean to my name and I drink too much Rosé wine. The little money I do accumulate to pay the rent comes from old residuals, poetry and favors to men. I have hope."

Hollywood was not interested in making the story of her life; it was too trite.

During World War II, Veronica Lake joined Rita Hayworth, Betty Grable and Marlene Dietrich as a favorite pin-up of GI's.

Although she was originally spotted by a Metro-Goldwyn-Mayer talent scout at the age of fifteen, after Constance (Connie) Ockleman was brought to Hollywood by her mother and stepfather, it was Paramount that finally signed her to a contract and changed her name to Veronica Lake.

Ronnie—as her drinking buddies called her—was unusual for Hollywood. She had only one ambition—to go back home to Oklahoma.

Unfortunately for Veronica, she became a quick success in Hollywood, becoming the top female box office attraction of 1942. Her performances in *Sullivan's Travels, I Married a Witch* and *So Proudly We Hail* showed her to be both a talented comedienne and a good dramatic actress. When she was paired with Alan Ladd in *This Gun for Hire*, the studio discovered they had a new romantic team on their hands and several more Ladd/Lake movies resulted.

But Lake's personal life was a shambles. She hated Hollywood and she hated the movies, but she was trapped by a vocation in which she was extremely successful. She tried to settle down, but marriage after marriage failed. She married three times and had three children, but her unhappy personal life began to affect her screen career and she became extremely temperamental, often drowning her sorrows in liquor as many actresses had before her. Her studio finally dropped her contract.

By the end of the 1950s, she was a hostess in a New York City cafe and appeared briefly as a replacement in an off-Broadway production of *Best Foot Forward*. Eventually, she published the story of her life, *Veronica*, which Hollywood celebrated and immediately forgot. She retreated to England, where she appeared on stage and married for the fourth time. Two years later, on July 7, 1973, in Burlington, Vermont, she died of hepatitis brought on by years of alcoholism. She was fifty-one.

Sue Lyon was a bright, beautiful child raised in an economically disadvantaged area of Los Angeles called Echo Park. Her father had died ten months after she was born in Davenport, Iowa, leaving her mother with five children. From the beginning, she modeled children's clothing to help support the family, finally moving into television in the role of the precocious child.

In 1960, an attractive, blonde, fourteen-year-old with seductive pale blue eyes, Sue had a ten minute interview with Stanley Kubrick and snapped up one of the most desired and talked about roles ever written: the part of the sexual nymphet opposite James Mason's smitten professor in the screen version of Vladimir Nabokov's novel *Lolita*.

Almost overnight, the whole world knew about Sue Lyon. Nabokov described her performance as "the perfect nymphet." She received critical acclaim for the part and played another teen-age temptress in *Night of the Iguana*. She continued to make about a film a year, including *Flim Flam Man, Seven Women* and *Tony Rome*.

At the age of seventeen, she married for the first time. She divorced within a year after the wedding. Another marriage and divorce followed. The nymphet of the 1960s was a mother in the 1970s, raising a daughter from her second marriage, when she met Gary (Cotton) Abramson. Abramson was an escaped convict from a Colorado prison, where he had been serving two concurrent twenty to forty year terms for murder and bank robbery. When he was captured and returned to prison, Sue corresponded and, in 1973, they were married in the prison yard at Canyon City. The marriage put an end to what career she had remaining. Finally, in 1974, she announced that she was divorcing Abramson because her marriage meant that she could no longer work in films.

Her career remained sporadic, but never again reached the high point at which it had started. Films like *Evel Knievel* (1972), *To Love Perhaps To Die (1976), Crash* and *End of the World (1978), The Astral Factor* and *Towing (1979), Alligator* (1981) and *The Invisible Strangler* (1985) kept reminding the world that Sue Lyon was alive and working, but they did little to raise her image or financial status.

Peter Sellers once said she had a "frightening natural, aggressive talent." Today, Sue Lyon lives quietly, coping with her life and her personal problems as best she can, her story of fame and success ending in relative obscurity.

CHAPTER 10

Where Nothing Is What It Seems

Robert Walker once said the first words he remembered hearing his mother say were "bad boy!" which made him feel inadequate, unwanted, unloved. "I was always trying to make an escape from life." Because he regularly got into trouble, at fourteen Walker was entered into the prestigious Davis San Diego Army and Navy Academy. He hated every minute of the strict regimen of having to carry himself straight as a ramrod and drill like a mindless tin soldier. He was a skinny, unhappy youth with weak eyes, plagued with acne, but then a kind of miracle occurred: one teacher recognized a rare sensitivity in the youngster and got him interested in acting. He played a plethora of parts and won prizes for his acting talent. Robert Walker found his niche and continued to study acting, including taking courses at the American Academy of Dramatic Arts.

That is where he met Phyllis Lee Isley, later to become famous as Jennifer Jones.

Phyllis was literally born in a trunk; her father owned a theatrical stock company. Robert was nineteen and penniless. Phyllis was eighteen, with a father who had some influence in the theatrical community. Both of them were talented and ambitious. Soon they were inseparable.

Robert and Phyllis married on the one year anniversary of their first meeting. The newlyweds received a Packard convertible from Phyllis's family as a wedding gift and the two decided to give Hollywood a try. Bob was certain that Phyl would take the movie town by storm. He was much less secure when it came to his own career. They arrived with $400 and letters of introduction from Phyllis's father to some of his friends.

On June 25, 1939, she signed a contract with Republic Pictures for $75 a week and was immediately cast as John Wayne's love interest in *New Frontier*—one week's work. That was all. Robert became a reader for the studios and did an occasional bit role. Disappointed, they sold the Packard and returned to New York.

Phyllis discovered that she was pregnant. Bob offered to give up acting to take care of her, but she would have none of that and Bob was hired for some great acting roles in radio dramas. Robert Jr. was born in 1940 and another son was born in 1941.

David O. Selznick was a major producer at Metro-Goldwyn-Mayer who was responsible for such hits as *A Tale of Two Cities, Anna Karenina, David Copperfield, Intermezzo, Gone With the Wind* and *Rebecca*. He had also discovered Ingrid Bergman.

Selznick heard Phyllis Walker read for the lead role in the movie, *Claudia*. During the audition, she became emotional, burst into tears and ran out of the room, sure that she had failed her chance at the part. However, Selznick stared after her, turned to his cohorts and said, "Sign her"—two words which would turn her wildest dreams into reality while Robert Walker's reality would become a nightmare. Although Dorothy McGuire eventually played the role of Claudia, Phyllis was signed to a contract.

Selznick decided to showcase his contract players in a month-long summer stock season in Santa Barbara, California and Phyllis had to fly to the West Coast at once. This was the first separation ever for the Walkers.

Bob turned twenty-three on October 14, 1941 and considered himself the luckiest guy in the world. He had the woman he loved, two healthy sons and an ironclad determination when it came to his work. It did not occur to him to worry about Selznick—a fortyish family man who was physically unattractive.

Phyllis was renamed Jennifer Jones and again traveled to the West Coast, this time to make a screen test for the title role of a fourteen-year-old girl in *The Song of Bernadette*. She was given the role—especially after everyone involved had been bombarded with calls and notes from Selznick.

Selznick wanted to create an aura of mystery around his latest discovery and detested spouses who interfered in his stars' careers—or even in their lives. Consequently, Bob and the boys were never mentioned in publicity releases about Jennifer Jones. But, in order to keep Bob busy, Selznick had him test and Walker was given a contract at Metro-Goldwyn-Mayer.

Bob proved to be sensational in *Bataan*, which starred Robert Taylor and he was immediately cast in other pictures. Meanwhile, Jennifer's star exploded and her part of Bernadette would win her an Academy Award for Best Actress.

Bob's first title role was for *See Here Private Hargrove* and he spontaneously decided to visit his wife on the set to share the happy news with her. He had never done that before. At the gate, he was turned down. "Sorry. Closed Set. Miss Jones cannot be disturbed," he was told.

Something had changed in their respective attitudes. He remained determined and enjoyed making his living as an actor, but she was becoming totally obsessed. It also became obvious that Selznick's feelings for Jennifer were deepening and that he wanted to possess her completely.

Then Selznick did a strange thing—he cast the couple as lovers in *Since You Went Away*. At the same time, Jennifer told Bob that it would be better if they separated. Bob was devastated. He was a person who had never been drunk or had ever shown any violent tendencies, but he checked into a hotel and got roaring drunk.

Production on the movie began on September 8, 1943. It had a shooting schedule of 127 days, during which Bob and Jennifer were lovers in the screenplay, although she disappeared during breaks. Bob's tension heightened. He had a motorcycle accident and was off the picture for a couple of weeks—a seemingly perfect opportunity for Selznick to replace him. He did not do so.

Bob's friends worried about the change in his personality. From being happy-go-lucky, he became morose, a shadow of his former self. He was still in love with Jennifer, but she rejected him. Selznick was so unappealing that when Hollywood stars played a popular party game of "Who is the last person in town you would go to bed with?" Marlene Dietrick's answer was a prompt, "David Selznick!"

The divorce was postponed until after the Oscar ceremonies. Bob, evidently a one-woman man, drank more and more and seemed to take no joy in anything, not even in the success he was experiencing in his career.

"Hollywood blew it," Bob said bitterly many times. "We would have been fine if we'd never gone to Hollywood."

Selznick, on the other hand, seemed determined to prove that he could have both his wife Irene and Jennifer Jones.

In 1944, a thin and haggard-looking Robert Walker made *The Clock* with Judy Garland and *Her Highness and the Bellboy* with June Allyson and Hedy Lamarr. He was only twenty-six, a terrific actor, but maritally shell-shocked and with a growing death wish. One night, he called newlyweds Judy Garland and Vincent Minnelli and drunkenly informed them that he was going to kill himself. They implored him to come to their house and, once there, listened patiently while he spouted his hatred for Hollywood and all it stood for.

On the last day of February, 1945, shooting began on *Duel in the Sun* for Jennifer Jones. The movie would continue for nine dramatic months. King Vidor directed, but David Selznick was on the set at all times, re-directing and putting Jennifer through hard times, mentally and physically.

Bob made *The Sailor Takes a Wife*. June Allyson did everything she could to help him, as did director Richard Whorf. Both believed in his abilities. They even arranged dates with some of Hollywood's most attractive women. Florence Pritchett, a model and writer from New York, seemed for a time to be able to dispel some of Bob's dark moods—at least until Friday, August 24, 1946. Hollywood newspaper headlines delivered the message: "The Selznicks, Wed Fifteen Years, Part."

Bob disappeared. Though he was in the middle of a filming, he jumped into his car and just kept driving. He returned a couple of days later. The romance with Florence was a casualty.

Asked to play composer Jerome Kern in *Till the Clouds Roll By*, Walker hesitated until Kern himself, encouraged by his wife, asked him. During the filming, Jerome Kern died—a death that Bob took very hard.

In August, 1946, Bob was restless and lonely. He had been drinking and his Chrysler sideswiped a bakery truck. Bob continued driving and the driver of the truck reported the incident to the police. Two days later, Bob entered a plea of hit-and-run driving and was sentenced to 180 days in jail. The sentence was suspended on the condition that Bob stay sober.

Hatred for Selznick—and ultimately Hollywood—began to consume Bob. When he went to see *Duel in the Sun*, he walked out in a rage after the rape scene. He began to hate his own roles, often disparaging *Song of Love*, and became contemptuous of the industry that he felt was responsible for his beloved Phyl deserting him.

He started *One Touch of Venus* with Ava Gardner and it became obvious that she decided to add young Walker to her conquests. He knew that she was involved with Howard Duff at the time, was shocked at her behavior and is supposed to have actually slapped his forward costar.

He continued drinking and began passing out. Shelley Winters became a good, close friend—not a date, but a pal who managed to cheer him up. He decided that he wanted to meet a nice, unglamorous girl "that nobody would want to take away from me." John Ford's twenty-five-year-old daughter, Barbara, fell in love with him and they began to spend all their time together, frequently on her father's yacht in Catalina. After six weeks, they decided to marry on July 3rd, but changed their minds at the last minute and cancelled, suddenly decided to marry on July 8th without telling their respective parents.

The marriage was a tragic mistake. Jennifer began calling the house more often after the marriage—she and Bob talked regularly because of their boys. In early August, Bob locked himself in his room for four days, refusing to come out. And things were to get worse. On August 14th, Bob went berserk and began beating Barbara. She managed to call her father; the marriage lasted less than six weeks. It was as if Bob was punishing Barbara, a thoroughly nice girl, for not being Jennifer.

During it all, he loved his sons and spent time with them, giving them the best education possible and expressing strong hopes that neither boy would ever turn to acting.

His drinking put his career into limbo. He listened eagerly to every piece of news about Jennifer. The papers were filled with reports that the Selznick empire was collapsing.

That October, Bob was again arrested as drunk and disorderly. Unflattering pictures were taken of him at the station, showing him thrusting his fist at policemen. Jennifer tried talking to him and pleaded that he take hold of himself for the sake of their sons. Her argument got through to Bob and he felt deep remorse. Dore Schary, the Metro chief, decided not to fire him, but demanded that he undergo treatment at the Menninger Clinic. Metro-Goldwyn-Mayer would foot the bill if Bob agreed. Bob agreed.

At the clinic, he was shocked to find that the doors were locked and there were bars on the windows. He used his acting ability to convince the doctors that he was in control of himself and received permission to spend one day outside. He headed straight for the nearest bar and put his fist through a glass-covered bulletin board. The police arrived. He returned to the clinic, no longer resisting treatment, but starting to talk, pouring out his despondency to his doctors.

Jennifer Jones started filming *Madame Bovary*—and quarreled frequently, often in public, with Selznick.

Bob was released from the Menninger Clinic in May and declared capable of working, unless such work was too strenuous. Schary cast him in *Please Believe Me* with Deborah Kerr. It seemed all right. Bob found a house in Malibu for himself and his sons and called it Rancho de Tres Haricots. His sons became the main focus in his life.

"I'm the driver, not the driven," he said in an interview. He seemed back to his normal self, even when Jennifer became Mrs. David Selznick on July 13th.

But when Jennifer and David wanted to move to Europe and take the boys with them, Bob narrowly escaped serious injury in a traffic accident which, however, was declared not to be his fault. The Selznicks decided against Europe. Although Bob began to date, he seemed reluctant to make any commitments. He made *Vengeance Valley* and became friends with Burt Lancaster.

By 1950, things looked better than ever for Robert Walker. Alfred Hitchcock offered him a role in *Strangers on a Train*—an excellent example of Hitchcock's famous "casting against type" technique. Bob was flattered. He was happy working for Hitchcock and Hitchcock was happy with him. In the picture, Bob's performance as the degenerate Bruno Anthony was just about perfect.

The early months of 1951 were good—but time was running out for Robert Walker.

Jennifer Jones suffered from depression following a miscarriage. Her career was at its lowest point in eight years. She began to withdraw more and more, preferring seclusion to parties. Selznick had severe financial problems.

Bob met Kay Scott, a former starlet, now a writer and

composer. She was a quiet, gentle woman.   The boys, Bobby and Michael, came for frequent and long visits.

Bob then began filming *My Son John*, an anti-communist melodrama. He himself was apolitical and was excited only by playing opposite Helen Hayes. Once the shooting started, he became unhappy with the director, whom he felt was heavy-handed and overdoing the political message at the expense of the subtlety of the plot line.

At this time there were no indications of any health or mental problems with Robert Walker.

The morning of August 28th was chilly; clouds and fog draped everything in a gray shroud. Bob slept late. His sons were away with friends. He may have been a bit restless and bored, but, when his business manager spoke with him by phone at 2:00 p.m., he seemed fine. No one knows what happened during the next four hours.

At six o'clock, the housekeeper called Bob's psychiatrist, saying that her employer was distraught and "out of control." But a friend, Jim Henaghan, dropped by for a drink and Bob seemed normal. Dr. Hacker, the psychiatrist, arrived as Henaghan was ready to leave. The doctor asked him to stay and help put Walker to bed. An associate of the psychiatrist arrived. Both doctors agreed that Bob needed a sedative—sodium amytal—to help him sleep. Bob refused the injection and ran outside in the rain. Henaghan ran after him and managed to bring him back inside and pinned him down on the bed. Bob was laughing. He was given the injection and passed out immediately. But Dr. Hacker noticed that something was wrong. Bob seemed to have stopped breathing. Hacker gave him artificial respiration while his associate called the fire department's emergency squad. Henaghan also hurried out, drove like a maniac and picked up another doctor whom he knew, one considered to be a brilliant internist. The three doctors did what they could—but Robert Walker was dead. He was not yet thirty-three years old.

Henaghan was in shock. He felt like a murderer and was unable to attend the funeral. The doctors repeated that Bob had been given the same dosage of sodium amytal before with no ill effects.

Jennifer Jones never publicly discussed Robert Walker.

Her career revived with the movie *Ruby Gentry*. Director King Vidor made David Selznick swear to stay away from the set before he would take the job. She went on to play many parts—the public loved her fragile quality. Friends frequently found her nervous and high-strung, but at least she was working.

In 1954, she gave birth to a daughter, Mary Jennifer.

David Selznick suffered five heart attacks in 1964 and died on June 23rd. Jennifer lived in seclusion with her young daughter. Later, she tried to do a play which turned out to be unsuccessful and no offers for work came her way.

On November 9, 1967, having received word that her friend Charles Bickford had died, her feelings of being unloved reached bottom. With a bottle of champagne and a bottle of Seconal, she checked into a Malibu Beach motel under the name of Phyllis Walker and called her physician. The police were alerted; they found her at the base of a cliff with the rising tide washing over her body. She did not seem to be breathing, but mouth-to-mouth resuscitation was successful.

In April 1971, a mutual friend arranged a blind date between Jennifer and Norton Simon. A month later, on May 30, 1971, she married the canned food millionaire. Simon himself was no stranger to tragedy. His life was rocked by the suicide, in 1969, of his thirty-one year old son, Robert Ellis Simon. Jennifer began traveling around the world, buying art treasures for Simon's unique and remarkable art collection. Although she had no formal art background, she is credited with initiating Simon's pursuit of Asian art and played a star role in auctions. She made one movie in 1974, *The Towering Inferno*. Her life seemed to be balanced until tragedy struck on May 11, 1976, when Mary Jennifer, then twenty-one years old, rode an elevator to the top of an office building in Los Angeles, stepped out onto the roof and jumped to her death.

From that point on, Jennifer Jones became a very private person. In 1989, she succeeded her husband as president of the Norton Simon Museum and donates large sums of money to mental health work.

Paul Kelly began his career playing juvenile leads on the New York stage. In 1917, when he was eighteen, he met a pretty Scottish lass named Dorothy Mackaye, who had also been an actress since childhood. Dorothy was an accomplished musical comedy performer as well.

Ten years later, Dorothy had married Ray Raymond, another musical comedy actor, and the two had moved to Hollywood. The year before, Paul Kelly had also moved West and had just finished a role in an Eddie Cantor movie *Unspecial Delivery*.

On Saturday, April 16, 1927, Kelly, an athletic young man, six feet tall and weighing 180 pounds, went to the Raymond house. Kelly wanted to settle a score with Raymond, who he felt was spreading untrue stories about him. "You are in love with my wife," accused Raymond.

The two men lunged at each other. Raymond's five year old daughter Valerie witnessed the fight. Raymond was felled twice by Kelly, who kicked his adversary and beat his head against the wall. Dorothy was not at home—she was out buying Easter eggs.

Raymond died on April 20th without having regained consciousness. The coroner's report indicated one fractured rib, one cracked rib, two contusions on the forehead, a damaged left eye, a bruised right shoulder, a bruised left forearm, bruised shins and a bruised chest and injury to the brain from pressure due to a severe hemorrhage on the right portion of the brain. The cause of death was listed as hypostatic pneumonia following extensive subdural hemorrhage on the right side of the brain. Acute alcoholism was given as a contributory cause.

Paul Kelly was arrested. He admitted that he was in

love with Dorothy Mackaye, but said that she did not return his feelings. There had been trouble between the two men for several months, which culminated in the fist fight, he said.

Kelly was sentenced to between one and ten years in jail for manslaughter.

Two years later, he was released from San Quentin and, two years after the release, he and Dorothy Mackaye married. His career was unaffected and Kelly was an extremely popular and busy movie actor until his death in 1956.

All performers and especially movie stars are vulnerable to one of the oldest confidence games in the world—false claims of assault or insult.

For example:

"He kissed me once. Then he told me how much prettier the moon was when seen through a porthole, and invited me to his cabin below."

"And then what happened?"

"I was on the bed, looking through the porthole."

"Did you resist?"

"Some. I kicked down a curtain beside the bed."

"Did you say anything?"

"I wanted him to leave me alone."

"Did you talk to him later?"

"I telephoned him . . . he asked me if I loved him. I said that naturally I hated him. I said my mother was going to prosecute him."

This was part of the actual trial testimony of Polly Satterle, one of the two teenage girls who charged Errol Flynn with statutory rape, which could have resulted in a lengthy jail term for him, and asked for damages in the amount of $100,000. After a sensational trial, the swashbuckling actor was acquitted. The jury pronounced him "not guilty," but Errol Flynn was guilty. He was guilty of poor judgment.

Testimony at the trial proved he had flirted with the plaintiffs, as he flirted with all women. Even as he went to court each day, he flirted with the young and pretty girl who sold cigarettes and newspapers in the courthouse foyer. The girl's name was Nora Eddington and, shortly after the trial, they married.

Popular leading men have traditionally been in danger of being victimized. Paternity suits have been brought toward many and few have publicly expressed thanks at being selected as possible fathers. "At my age, it is a great compliment," remarked an aging Wallace Beery, one of the few exceptions to the rule.

One reason Elvis Presley always traveled with bodyguards was so they could prove that any such accusations against him were false.

Clark Gable did not escape blackmailers. A shrewd composite picture, showing him fondling a young girl, was actually a doctored shot of his head superimposed on another man's body.

When Charlie Chaplin wed eighteen-year-old Oona O'Neill in 1944, he was entangled in a paternity suit by his young "protégé," Joan Barry. The trial produced some of the spiciest court testimony on record.

George Maharis was on location for the hit television series "Route 66." In this small town, a girl told her boyfriend that Maharis had made a pass at her. Unknowingly, when the actor went to relax and have a beer in a local cafe, he was accosted by the angry young man—and, before long, hemmed in by an upset crowd. Maharis did the only sensible thing—he ran for his life.

Veteran screen idol Francis X. Bushman once had to jump over the back fence of a movie studio to escape from a husband who thought he was having an affair with his wife.

If female fans don't go a bit crazy over a leading man, he is in trouble. When they do, he could also be in trouble.

Cary Grant was in his New York hotel suite when he got the following phone call.

"May I speak to Mr. Grant," said a nervous female

voice. "Tell him I'm a young actress who would like some advice."

"This is Mr. Grant," Cary said, in his friendly way. "What can I do for you?"

"You can't fool me," said the girl. "I understand very well that you're not Cary Grant. Tell him from me that I think he's a awful snob who won't come to the phone."

"My dear young lady," he said patiently, "this is Cary Grant."

"Sure, you sound a little like him. That's why he employed you, huh? I know damn well that he'd think he's too good to speak to somebody like me!"

Sometimes, it's hard to win with fans.

Tom Neal's life was stranger and more dramatic than his career.

He excelled as a boxer in college, tried the stage and appeared in three Broadway flops in a row, and received his law degree from Harvard University in 1938. Neal then went to Hollywood and was given minor parts at Metro-Goldwyn-Mayer.

He played movie tough guys throughout the '40s and '50s without much acclaim, but received plenty of attention in 1951 when he broke Franchot Tone's nose in a brawl over Barbara Payton. Tone, the perfect matinee idol of his time, four times married and an ex-husband of Joan Crawford, married Payton when he was released from the hospital—where he required plastic surgery to fix his nose. Months later, they divorced and she returned to Neal, whom she wed not long after that. Even though she continued to work in films for a while, the scandal harmed Neal's career and he ended up as a gardener in Palm Springs.

After their divorce, he went bankrupt, failing to start a successful landscaping business. A second marriage ended in divorce. In 1965, he shot and killed his third wife. He claimed it had been an accident, but was sentenced to six years in jail. Eight months after his release in 1972, fifty-eight year old Tom Neal died of congestive heart failure.

There is a Hollywood legend concerning John Barrymore's "last appearance."

When "The Great Profile" died in May, 1942, doctors stated the cause of death as cirrhosis of the liver plus a virtual catalogue of other diseases of the hard-living man: kidney failure, chronic gastritis, ulceration of the esophagus, hardening of the arteries and chronic eczema.

Artist John Decker was with Barrymore when he died. The two and Errol Flynn made up a trio of close friends who quoted Shakespeare and spoke ribaldly about the ladies they had bedded.

When Decker told Flynn about the great actor's death, Flynn burst into tears. "It couldn't have been worse, had it been my own father." Decker had sketched their dying friend and had taken care of the funeral arrangements before going to Flynn's house with the sad news. A number of other friends—close buddies of John Barrymore, including W.C. Fields and Gene Fowler—gathered for an informal wake. Flynn cried, then blew his nose and left to keep a previous rendezvous.

Legend and truth can form a strange mixture. There are two scenarios as to what actually happened that night.

Here is one version: Barrymore's drinking buddies went to the mortuary and somehow managed to "borrow" the body and bring it to the home of director Raoul Walsh. When Walsh, who had visited the mortuary earlier, walked in his front door, he found Barrymore sitting in his living room holding a martini. Certainly Walsh had seen Barrymore dead drunk before . . .

The second version of the story is one that Flynn himself helped to perpetuate: Barrymore's drinking buddies were sitting in Errol Flynn's house—after Flynn had left—when director Raoul Walsh had a morbid idea, "Let's bring the old boy back here."

They drove to the mortuary and managed to "borrow" John Barrymore's body for a couple of hours. When they returned to the house, Flynn's butler did a double take and pointed out that Barrymore didn't look well at all. They put the corpse in a sitting position—not easy, since rigor mortis had set in—in the chair Barrymore considered his own and where he often sat telling his remarkable stories.

When Flynn returned from his assignation and pressed the button to turn the lights on—he found himself staring into the face of Barrymore. "His eyes were closed. He looked puffed, white, bloodless. They hadn't embalmed him yet. I let out a delirious scream. I turned to run out of the house. I intended getting into my car to flee down the hill away from my place, away from myself."

Screaming, Flynn hid behind an oleander bush on the patio. Welsh and the others tried to calm him down—between fits of laughter. "Easy, boy—it's just a gag."

No mortuary would have allowed Barrymore's buddies to "borrow" his body, but Barrymore himself would have probably enjoyed this macabre farewell.

The most remarkable thing about Errol Flynn's death in 1959 may be that it did not happen earlier. Flynn was a man who lived on the edge, one who took more chances than ten others in a lifetime.

When he made *Gentleman Jim* in 1942, which included a number of boxing scenes, Flynn had a mild heart attack. The doctors repeated what army doctors had said before: his heart was in as bad shape as his lungs. Either could give out fairly soon.

During the filming of *Northern Pursuit* in 1943, he collapsed on the set, and it was discovered that he had contacted tuberculosis. The public relations department at Warner Brothers kept the nature of his illness very quiet—aided by a press corps who was always fascinated by the colorful actor. In later years, the tabloids and scandal sheets had a field day reporting Flynn's real or rumored escapades, but, in 1943, Warner's biggest male star could not be revealed to be consumptive.

Flynn also had occasional bouts with malaria, one of

the legacies from his youthful years in New Guinea. Since he did most of his own stunts in his movies, he suffered many bruises and broken bones. Strangely, even though he performed many of his own stunts, Flynn was actually plagued by a fear of heights.

A legendary womanizer, who reportedly hated his mother all his life, Flynn married three times: to Lili Damita, whom he called Tiger Lil, Nora Eddington and Patrice Wymore. He fathered four children, Sean, Deirdre, Rory and Arnella, and was a better father than is obvious from articles written about him.

When he was forty-eight and played John Barrymore with loving perfection (he was also a finer and more serious actor than some critics credited him) in *Too Much, Too Soon*, he met a bubbly teenager, Beverly Aadland, whom he dubbed Woodsie, short for "Little Wood Nymph." His letters to her while he was in Africa filming *The Roots of Heaven*, show a strong, caring man.

He wrote his autobiography, *My Wicked, Wicked Ways*, again revealing himself as an articulate, thinking man, even though his body at that time was ravaged by the years of often self-inflicted punishment.

He journeyed to Cuba to meet with Fidel Castro, saying that he would write a book about the Latin dictator. There, he also filmed some location footage for a motion picture entitled *Cuban Rebel Girls*, in which he would play himself as a war correspondent. Flynn also wanted to provide Beverly Aadland with the chance to start a film career.

His health steadily declined and doctors said he would be lucky to live another year. "Modify your habits or take the consequences," he was told. "I'll take the consequences," said Errol Flynn, true to style.

And so he did, on October 14, 1959. He was in Vancouver, Canada, with Beverly, meeting with a couple who were buying his beloved 120-foot boat, the Zaca. They all went to the home of Dr. George Gould, who was having a few friends over. The doctor examined Flynn, gave him an injection and told him to lie down. Flynn said that he would prefer some interesting conversation and, for two hours, he entertained the guests with fabulous stories about Hollywood and its people. Then, suddenly, he declared that he would lie down. Walking toward the bedroom, he collapsed. He had suffered a massive heart attack and was rushed to the hospital, where he died only minutes after arrival. The death certificate read Flynn died from coronary thrombosis complicated by a hardening of the arteries, degeneration of the liver and infection of the lower intestine. His body was that of someone much older than a man of fifty—but then, Errol Flynn had crammed more than one lifetime into that half century.

Lon Chaney, the "Man of a Thousand Faces," spent his years on earth playing characters with severe handicaps.

For the part of Quasimoto in *The Hunchback of Notre Dame*, he arrived at the studio at 4:30 in the morning to prepare himself for the day's filming. He modeled a hideous putty face by inserting snagged false teeth and forming shaggy eyebrows, hair by hair. A piece of fish skin was put inside his eyelid and held in place by collodion to create the sightless eye. Then, he harnessed himself with leather shoulder pads and a heavy breastplate of steel. From front to back, between his legs, a broad leather strap was hooked to the shoulder pads and laced to the breastplate with leather thongs which were pulled taut until his own spine bent in the hunchback's terrible curve. Over this, Chaney wore a suit of heavy rubber to conceal the harness.

Doctors warned him that staying in that position more than twenty minutes could be potentially damaging. Often he stayed in it an hour. Was such pure torture necessary for the part?

His answer was, "Not for acting, for the truth!" He *was* a hunchback; he did not play at it.

When he played the legless man in *The Penalty*,

Chaney acted the part on his knees. His lower legs were bent up and bound to his thighs, after which his knees were fitted into stump shoes.

Lon Chaney was the son of deaf mute parents and grew up in silence. He worked his way traveling with a comedy repertoire company when a fifteen year old girl named Cleva Creighton answered an ad for chorus girls. Three days later, they were married. Two years later, their son Creighton—later known as Lon Chaney Jr.—was born

Cleva had a sweet voice and could sing an Irish ballad with feeling. For a while, she drew considerably more attention than Chaney did. Unhappiness plagued the couple, and she began to drink. Chaney was jealous and believed that Cleva was an unfaithful wife.

One night, as he came off the stage, still in clown makeup and costume, Cleva fell at his feet. She had taken poison. All night, doctors fought for her life while the clown stood by silently, watching. At dawn, when he knew she would live, he left—and never went back.

He took their son with him.

The poison Cleva had taken destroyed her vocal chords. She could never sing again. She had no money. Cleva Creighton Chaney worked as a cook at a sugar beet ranch near Oxnard, California. Lon Chaney died of throat cancer when he was forty-three, having never mentioned her—until his last will and testament was read. He left her one dollar. Chaney had re-married, this time to Hazel Hastings, whose first husband ironically had been a man without legs.

You don't have to be crazy, but it helps; so goes the old saying about Hollywood. One of its strangest characters was German-American director William Dieterle, who made movies such as *The Story of Louis Pasteur, Juarez, The Life of Emile Zola, A Midsummer Night's Dream* and *Salome* during the golden age of Hollywood. A talented man, totally guided by astrology, Dieterle refused to walk on a set if the heavens produced unfavorable signs. He directed wearing black gloves. That, in combination with his pointed head, pasty white complexion and matted, inky-black hair, made him appear to be more like a resident of Transylvania than California. He lived up to that image by inhabiting a castle-like place—complete with dark woods, antlers on the walls, and Biedermeier furniture. He thrived in the rather oppressive, gloomy milieu.

The best little whorehouse in town, nestled high in the Hollywood hills, was a spacious Greek-revival structure with stately columns, wide porches and even a porte-cochere. It featured a well-manicured lawn in front and a topiary garden in back. Madam Mae, herself resembling Mae West, reigned with a firm hand over a large stable of girls, all look-alikes of stars.

While a Greta Garbo or Katharine Hepburn was hard to find, there was a Barbara Stanwyck, a Carole Lombard, an Alice Faye, an Irene Dunne, a Joan Crawford, a Claudette Colbert, a Janet Gaynor, a Myrna Loy and a Ginger Rogers.

It was a classy place, complete with a French chef to whip up delicacies for the fortification of the customers.

The basement housed the makeup, hair and wardrobe departments. Clothes were bought from studios, costumes were copied from movies and a married couple (she was a hairdresser; he was a makeup artist) created a bevy of likenesses of popular actresses.

On occasion, movies were screened, and the girls read the trade papers regularly, keeping up with the current activities of their respective star, so that they could speak knowledgeably about movie parts, co-stars and habits.

It was a place in which to live out your fantasies. Where else could it have happened, but in the Hollywood of yesterday.

Dennis Hopper is proof some Hollywood stories have happy endings.

He has done it all: cult movie star, award winning director, drug abuser, bad boy, good boy. During his thirty-four year career, Dennis Hopper has veered from being the toast of Hollywood to prolonged periods as a cinematic outcast with frightening regularity. Indeed, he has been to hell and back.

"I should be dead," he admits. And it is something of a miracle that he lived past thirty. Today, in his middle fifties, he looks good and has a young wife and a baby to round out a productive life.

Hopper was an early achiever. At the age of nineteen, he played with James Dean in both *Rebel Without a Cause* and *Giant*, but an argument on the set of a 1958 western *From Hell to Texas* closed the doors on any good film offers, until he bounced back into the limelight with the classic *Easy Rider* in 1969. Never one to take the soft option, Hopper blew mainstream credibility by directing *The Last Movie*, a wonderfully obscure film that so outraged his backers that he was forced back into an exile of drugs, firearms (he was busted in 1975 for allegedly running wild in a public square with a loaded .375 Magnum), straitjackets, psychiatric wards and substance abuse programs.

When Hopper arrived in Cuernavaca, Mexico, in 1983, for the filming of *Jungle Fever*, he ran naked through the streets until he was nabbed by the police. He was shipped back to Los Angeles and put into a psychiatric hospital. "For several months, he was a total zombie. He was paralyzed. He was used by the doctors as a warning example of where and how a drug user may end up. Then he slowly recovered and hooked up with Alcoholics Anonymous. A year later, he was acting all over the place with astounding and reverberating success," said one of Hopper's friends.

He did, indeed, perform a remarkable turn-around and got back on the winning track in 1986 when he played the Oscar-nominated alcoholic, basketballing dad in *Hoosiers* and the sexually-warped, sadistic Frank in David Lynch's *Blue Velvet*. Since then, Hopper has been busy both behind the camera (*Colors*, *The Hot Spot*) and in front of it. Sober since 1984, he is once again much in demand both as an actor and a director.

How did a man whose name was once synonymous with drugs and booze do it? And how did he get to that wild and crazy spot in the first place?

"All the people I admired were alcoholics and drug addicts: John Barrymore and painter Albert Decker, W.C. Fields and Charlie Parker. Then there were the writers: Baudelaire, Verlaine, Rimbaud and Edgar Allen Poe. I felt it was part of the game and that's how I justified it.

"I never hid my drinking. I never hid my drugs. I was not a sneaky guy. People in the press used to ask me about drugs and I'd say, 'I only do drugs to cover up the fact that I'm an alcoholic.' I used to like to make them laugh. I went on until I hit bottom. I went insane, you know. I started hearing voices and seeing space people.

"I was locked away in my room with a gun, a crazy, paranoid schizophrenic out of his mind. I'd isolated myself so much from the world that it's amazing I ever came back. It's amazing I have any mind left. It's amazing that I'm not dead, really.

"How I did it? I had no choice."

It is indeed amazing—and a testament of hope to human willpower and survival.

Epilogue

Fantasy and Illusion

Doubles, shadows and mirrors fascinate moviemakers with symbolic imagination, balancing on the borderline to the unconscious, the unknown, the almost or completely supernatural. Think of a Cocteau movie with its shadow play, scary surprises, unsuspected events, identity changes ... Imagine then that it is a normal day in Hollywood and suddenly you are lifted out of the ordinary and find yourself inside such a movie—chills along the spine, goose pimples and all.

It happened one day in 1966 at Twentieth Century-Fox Studios. Without warning, reality became blurred to this writer.

A feature was being shot and I roamed a bit aimlessly, stepping carefully over thick cables, my eye on the red lights which demanded absolute silence. The occasion for the visit was a scheduled interview with director Ralph Nelson. Between shots, we chatted about the movie as an art form, its possibilities, often the movies have shown the fascination of the mirror ... how we, as the audience, identify with the figures on the screen. We see a Marlon Brando, an Elizabeth Taylor breathe, we are close—for a moment we become them.

An interesting and highly theoretical observation as we were talking about moments of identification. Most of us, as we leave the dark theater, become ourselves. Life is one thing and a couple of hours at the movies just a short-lived experience.

Among the hot spotlights, ringling wires and technicians stood a group of extras, a profession on the lowest rung of the Hollywood ladder. Sometimes extras are just referred to as "atmosphere." One woman stood a short distance apart from the others—one extra among many. There was something vaguely familiar about her. She stood very still, staring toward one almost completely dark corner of the sound stage.

One of the ever-present studio publicists noticed my glance, touched my arm and whispered, "That woman—she was Marilyn Monroe's stand-in."

When the woman took her place among the others in front of the camera, I had a chance to study her—a woman with a Monroe-like hairdo, with Monroe's way of walking and (it was revealed later) Monroe's way of speaking. She had adopted a typical Monroe facial expression as well, that of a little girl toward whom somebody has behaved meanly. It seemed somewhat out of place on the forty-plus face. Seeing this woman was like seeing an older, deteriorated Marilyn Monroe.

"Her name is Evelyn Moriarty," I was told. "She lives in the past. Every 4th of August, on Monroe's death, she puts masses of flowers on Marilyn's grave at Westwood Memorial Park. Speak one ill word about Marilyn and she becomes a tigress."

I approached the woman. She had walked closer toward the dark corner as if pulled there by an invisible force. Her way of greeting, the slight bow of the head, was grotesquely like Marilyn Monroe's. She pointed dramatically toward the corner.

"There was a swimming pool right here. I was her double. It was a Friday. June 1st. Her birthday."

No name. Just "her."

"We had been working late and she was in a hurry to get to the stadium where she was to open the baseball season. You know, throw the first ball. She walked out of here in the clothes she wore for the movie. That was the last time she stood in front of a movie camera."

The woman turned her back to me as if ready to burst into tears.

"On Monday, her secretary called George Zukor, the producer (actually the director) and said that she didn't feel good. She had a fever most days. Anyhow, the script wasn't right for her. Dean (Martin) was nice, though. He got her a beautiful birthday cake. On Tuesday, they stopped the movie and tore up her contract. And on August 4th she died."

The memories seemed close there on sound stage number 14 where Monroe began filming her last movie, *Something's Got To Give* and was fired due to "lack of discipline." The movie was rewritten, its title changed to *Move Over Darling* and filmed starring Doris Day.

"What do you want to know?" the woman asked abruptly. "I don't know what to say. Ask me something."

I uttered the first question that occurred to me. "What exactly did you do as Marilyn Monroe's double?"

"I took her place during the setting of the lights—it takes a long time to get it right—so she would be fresh and pretty when it was time for a take. I was dressed exactly like her. Same hair color, same hairdo. There were always two identical wardrobes, one for her, one for me. Every time she changed clothes, I changed clothes. I replaced her in long shots, too. You know, shots from a distance. And sometimes, when she had to be dressed in a bikini, because she didn't like that."

"She didn't?"

"No. Of course, she was as beautiful as everybody says, but first and foremost she was a human being. A shy human being. She felt most comfortable in a kimono and without makeup. But she knew that she had to act like a sex symbol for the sake of audiences. She did not like it, but she did her duty. She had to look all the time as if she wanted to go to bed with every man in sight. She hated it."

"In how many movies did you work as her stand-in?"

"Three. Her last three movies. Did you know that her stand-in in earlier movies died within two weeks after she died? My first movie with her was *Let's Make Love* with Yves Montand. There I took over her lines too. For rehearsals, I mean. Yves had trouble with the English language and took too long, so I learned the lines and rehearsed with Yves. When he knew his lines, Marilyn took my place."

Marilyn took my place.

That's when it happened. The woman bit her thumb lightly, as was Marilyn's habit. One hand rested on her hip. As she stood there in the twilight of a corner of a studio sound stage, she seemed to assume Marilyn's identity.

I asked a question quickly. Did she work on *The Misfits*, Monroe's last completed film?

"Of course," she answered slowly in Monroe's slight drawl. "We filmed in Reno. I had a stand-in myself in a couple of scenes. I don't know how to ride."

What about John Huston, the director? I wanted to keep her talking, to let reality back in.

"He's wonderful! Fascinating! Very much a man, a real man."

There was an insinuating little smile, an imitation—or parody.

"And Arthur Miller?"

Her facial expression changed. She threw her hair back and let a suspicious side glance travel over me.

"Seriously and honestly, I don't understand how Arthur could . . . how could he?"

"What?"

"That play!"

(She was referring to *After the Fall*, where the lead, Maggie, is more than a little reminiscent of Marilyn. The play was widely discussed and divided movie people and theater critics into two camps. Otto Preminger said, in a television interview, that he felt Arthur Miller had shown bad taste. Elia Kazan opined, "Who had more right to analyze Marilyn than Miller?")

"She never defended herself," the woman exclaimed. Tears edged her voice. "I heard that Arthur made up a lot of things about her. He shouldn't have written that play. She tried to better herself. Always. But if she had been alive, she wouldn't have been angry with him. I know that. She'd have said, 'It doesn't matter, Arthur. I forgive you.'"

Again the woman fused with the fantasy. In one breathless sentence, she confided that she and Marilyn had "the exact same childhood, no parents, growing up in orphanages and foster homes."

She sighed and straightened her back as if she were carrying an invisible burden. "It was a terrible responsibility to be Marilyn. She told me her dreams—as when she dreamt she stood in a church, completely naked, and all the people were lying at her feet.

"She wanted to hide and often did—in a hospital or a restroom. If she was in a restaurant and didn't feel welcome—it happened often—she excused herself and went to the ladies room. There she could sit an hour. Or longer.

"Nobody knew her. They write all kinds of stories about her, but nobody knew her. She was terribly lonely. She had no real friends. Everybody used her. When she died all alone in her hacienda, as she called her home, my life ended, too. Nobody gave me a job. I said hello to people I had known and called by their first name and they looked right through me. I was not allowed to give interviews. They don't understand me . . . they don't know me, either. I'm alone, too.

"We understood each other. We couldn't go to Clark's funeral. Nobody would have understood the special feeling—how truly sorry we were. We learned to smile when sad.

"There are very few people one can trust."

She turned toward me and went through another metamorphosis. She became haughty, a big star—the identification was complete.

"I can't say any more. I'm not allowed to say any more. They are writing my life story in London. Good-bye."

She turned abruptly on her heels and walked toward the iron door. It was Marilyn Monroe's hip-swinging walk. Slowly, I followed her through the door and saw Evelyn Moriarity walk off—pathetic figure, a shadow, an unreal double. Marilyn Monroe was dead, but her stand-in, her double in the world of illusions, carried on.